Revolutionary Innovations of AI Driverless Cars

Practical Advances in Artificial Intelligence and Machine Learning

Dr. Lance B. Eliot, MBA, PhD

ISBN: 0578422239
ISBN-13: 978-0578422237

DEDICATION

To my incredible son, Michael, and my incredible daughter, Lauren.

Forest fortuna adiuvat (from the Latin; good fortune favors the brave).

CONTENTS

Lance B. Eliot

ACKNOWLEDGMENTS

I have been the beneficiary of advice and counsel by many friends, colleagues, family, investors, and many others. I want to thank everyone that has aided me throughout my career. I write from the heart and the head, having experienced first-hand what it means to have others around you that support you during the good times and the tough times.

To Warren Bennis, one of my doctoral advisors and ultimately a colleague, I offer my deepest thanks and appreciation, especially for his calm and insightful wisdom and support.

To Mark Stevens and his generous efforts toward funding and supporting the USC Stevens Center for Innovation.

To Lloyd Greif and the USC Lloyd Greif Center for Entrepreneurial Studies for their ongoing encouragement of founders and entrepreneurs.

To Peter Drucker, William Wang, Aaron Levie, Peter Kim, Jon Kraft, Cindy Crawford, Jenny Ming, Steve Milligan, Chis Underwood, Frank Gehry, Buzz Aldrin, Steve Forbes, Bill Thompson, Dave Dillon, Alan Fuerstman, Larry Ellison, Jim Sinegal, John Sperling, Mark Stevenson, Anand Nallathambi, Thomas Barrack, Jr., and many other innovators and leaders that I have met and gained mightily from doing so.

Thanks to Ed Trainor, Kevin Anderson, James Hickey, Wendell Jones, Ken Harris, DuWayne Peterson, Mike Brown, Jim Thornton, Abhi Beniwal, Al Biland, John Nomura, Eliot Weinman, John Desmond, and many others for their unwavering support during my career.

And most of all thanks as always to Michael and Lauren, for their ongoing support and for having seen me writing and heard much of this material during the many months involved in writing it. To their patience and willingness to listen.

Lance B. Eliot

INTRODUCTION

This is a book that provides the newest innovations and the latest Artificial Intelligence (AI) advances about the emerging nature of AI-based autonomous self-driving driverless cars. Via recent advances in Artificial Intelligence (AI) and Machine Learning (ML), we are nearing the day when vehicles can control themselves and will not require and nor rely upon human intervention to perform their driving tasks (or, that <u>allow</u> for human intervention, but only *require* human intervention in very limited ways).

Similar to my other related books, which I describe in a moment and list the chapters in the Appendix A of this book, I am particularly focused on those advances that pertain to self-driving cars. The phrase "autonomous vehicles" is often used to refer to any kind of vehicle, whether it is ground-based or in the air or sea, and whether it is a cargo hauling trailer truck or a conventional passenger car. Though the aspects described in this book are certainly applicable to all kinds of autonomous vehicles, I am focused more so here on cars.

Indeed, I am especially known for my role in aiding the advancement of self-driving cars, serving currently as the Executive Director of the Cybernetic Self-Driving Cars Institute.. In addition to writing software, designing and developing systems and software for self-driving cars, I also speak and write quite a bit about the topic. This book is a collection of some of my more advanced essays. For those of you that might have seen my essays posted elsewhere, I have updated them and integrated them into this book as one handy cohesive package.

You might be interested in companion books that I have written that provide additional key innovations and fundamentals about self-driving cars. Those books are entitled **"Introduction to Driverless Self-Driving Cars," "Advances in AI and Autonomous Vehicles: Cybernetic Self-Driving Cars," "Self-Driving Cars: "The Mother of All AI Projects," "Innovation and Thought Leadership on Self-Driving Driverless Cars," "New Advances in AI Autonomous Driverless Self-Driving Cars,"** and **"Autonomous Vehicle Driverless Self-Driving Cars and**

Artificial Intelligence," **"Transformative Artificial Intelligence Driverless Self-Driving Cars,"** **"Disruptive Artificial Intelligence and Driverless Self-Driving Cars,** and "State-of-the-Art AI Driverless Self-Driving Cars," and **"Top Trends in AI Self-Driving Cars,"** and **"AI Innovations and Self-Driving Cars,"** **"Crucial Advances for AI Driverless Cars,"** **"Sociotechnical Insights and AI Driverless Cars,"** **"Pioneering Advances for AI Driverless Cars"** and **"Leading Edge Trends for AI Driverless Cars,"** **"The Cutting Edge of AI Autonomous Cars"** and **"The Next Wave of AI Self-Driving Cars"** and **"Revolutionary Innovations of AI Self-Driving Cars"** (they are all available via Amazon). See Appendix A of this herein book to see a listing of the chapters covered in those three books.

For the introduction here to this book, I am going to borrow my introduction from those companion books, since it does a good job of laying out the landscape of self-driving cars and my overall viewpoints on the topic. The remainder of the book is all new material that does not appear in the companion books.

INTRODUCTION TO SELF-DRIVING CARS

This is a book about self-driving cars. Someday in the future, we'll all have self-driving cars and this book will perhaps seem antiquated, but right now, we are at the forefront of the self-driving car wave. Daily news bombards us with flashes of new announcements by one car maker or another and leaves the impression that within the next few weeks or maybe months that the self-driving car will be here. A casual non-technical reader would assume from these news flashes that in fact we must be on the cusp of a true self-driving car.

Here's a real news flash: We are still quite a distance from having a true self-driving car. It is years to go before we get there.

Why is that? Because a true self-driving car is akin to a moonshot. In the same manner that getting us to the moon was an incredible feat, likewise can it be said for achieving a true self-driving car. Anybody that suggests or even brashly states that the true self-driving car is nearly here should be viewed with great skepticism. Indeed, you'll see that I often tend to use the word "hogwash" or "crock" when I assess much of the decidedly *fake news* about self-driving cars. Those of us on the inside know that what is often reported to the outside is malarkey. Few of the insiders are willing to say so. I have no such hesitation.

Indeed, I've been writing a popular blog post about self-driving cars and hitting hard on those that try to wave their hands and pretend that we are on the imminent verge of true self-driving cars. For many years, I've been known as the AI Insider. Besides writing about AI, I also develop AI software. I do what I describe. It also gives me insights into what others that are doing AI are really doing versus what it is said they are doing.

Many faithful readers had asked me to pull together my insightful short essays and put them into another book, which you are now holding in your hands.

For those of you that have been reading my essays over the years, this collection not only puts them together into one handy package, I also updated the essays and added new material. For those of you that are new to the topic of self-driving cars and AI, I hope you find these essays approachable and informative. I also tend to have a writing style with a bit of a voice, and so you'll see that I am times have a wry sense of humor and also like to poke at conformity.

As a former professor and founder of an AI research lab, I for many years wrote in the formal language of academic writing. I published in referred journals and served as an editor for several AI journals. This writing here is not of the nature, and I have adopted a different and more informal style for these essays. That being said, I also do mention from time-to-time more rigorous material on AI and encourage you all to dig into those deeper and more formal materials if so interested.

I am also an AI practitioner. This means that I write AI software for a living. Currently, I head-up the Cybernetics Self-Driving Car Institute, where we are developing AI software for self-driving cars. I am excited to also report that my son, also a software engineer, heads-up our Cybernetics Self-Driving Car Lab. What I have helped to start, and for which he is an integral part, ultimately he will carry long into the future after I have retired. My daughter, a marketing whiz, also is integral to our efforts as head of our Marketing group. She too will carry forward the legacy now being formulated.

For those of you that are reading this book and have a penchant for writing code, you might consider taking a look at the open source code available for self-driving cars. This is a handy place to start learning how to develop AI for self-driving cars. There are also many new educational courses spring forth.

There is a growing body of those wanting to learn about and develop self-driving cars, and a growing body of colleges, labs, and other avenues by which you can learn about self-driving cars.

This book will provide a foundation of aspects that I think will get you ready for those kinds of more advanced training opportunities. If you've already taken those classes, you'll likely find these essays especially interesting as they offer a perspective that I am betting few other instructors or faculty offered to you. These are challenging essays that ask you to think beyond the conventional about self-driving cars.

THE MOTHER OF ALL AI PROJECTS

In June 2017, Apple CEO Tim Cook came out and finally admitted that Apple has been working on a self-driving car. As you'll see in my essays, Apple was enmeshed in secrecy about their self-driving car efforts. We have only been able to read the tea leaves and guess at what Apple has been up to. The notion of an iCar has been floating for quite a while, and self-driving engineers and researchers have been signing tight-lipped Non-Disclosure Agreements (NDA's) to work on projects at Apple that were as shrouded in mystery as any military invasion plans might be.

Tim Cook said something that many others in the Artificial Intelligence (AI) field have been saying, namely, the creation of a self-driving car has got to be the mother of all AI projects. In other words, it is in fact a tremendous moonshot for AI. If a self-driving car can be crafted and the AI works as we hope, it means that we have made incredible strides with AI and that therefore it opens many other worlds of potential breakthrough accomplishments that AI can solve.

Is this hyperbole? Am I just trying to make AI seem like a miracle worker and so provide self-aggrandizing statements for those of us writing the AI software for self-driving cars? No, it is not hyperbole. Developing a true self-driving car is really, really, really hard to do. Let me take a moment to explain why. As a side note, I realize that the Apple CEO is known for at times uttering hyperbole, and he had previously said for example that the year 2012 was "the mother of all years," and he had said that the release of iOS 10 was "the mother of all releases" – all of which does suggest he likes to use the handy "mother of" expression. But, I assure you, in terms of true self-driving cars, he has hit the nail on the head. For sure.

When you think about a moonshot and how we got to the moon, there are some identifiable characteristics and those same aspects can be applied to creating a true self-driving car. You'll notice that I keep putting the word "true" in front of the self-driving car expression. I do so because as per my essay about the various levels of self-driving cars, there are some self-driving cars that are only somewhat of a self-driving car. The somewhat versions are ones that require a human driver to be ready to intervene. In my view, that's not a true self-driving car. A true self-driving car is one that requires no human driver intervention at all. It is a car that can entirely undertake via automation the driving task without any human driver needed. This is the essence of what is known as a Level 5 self-driving car. We are currently at the Level 2 and Level 3 mark, and not yet at Level 5.

Getting to the moon involved aspects such as having big stretch goals, incremental progress, experimentation, innovation, and so on. Let's review how this applied to the moonshot of the bygone era, and how it applies to the self-driving car moonshot of today.

Big Stretch Goal

Trying to take a human and deliver the human to the moon, and bring them back, safely, was an extremely large stretch goal at the time. No one knew whether it could be done. The technology wasn't available yet. The cost was huge. The determination would need to be fierce. Etc. To reach a Level 5 self-driving car is going to be the same. It is a big stretch goal. We can readily get to the Level 3, and we are able to see the Level 4 just up ahead, but a Level 5 is still an unknown as to if it is doable. It should eventually be doable and in the same way that we thought we'd eventually get to the moon, but when it will occur is a different story.

Incremental Progress

Getting to the moon did not happen overnight in one fell swoop. It took years and years of incremental progress to get there. Likewise for self-driving cars. Google has famously been striving to get to the Level 5, and pretty much been willing to forgo dealing with the intervening levels, but most of the other self-driving car makers are doing the incremental route. Let's get a good Level 2 and a somewhat Level 3 going. Then, let's improve the Level 3 and get a somewhat Level 4 going. Then, let's improve the Level 4 and finally arrive at a Level 5. This seems to be the prevalent way that we are going to achieve the true self-driving car.

Experimentation

You likely know that there were various experiments involved in perfecting the approach and technology to get to the moon. As per making incremental progress, we first tried to see if we could get a rocket to go into space and safety return, then put a monkey in there, then with a human, then we went all the way to the moon but didn't land, and finally we arrived at the mission that actually landed on the moon. Self-driving cars are the same way. We are doing simulations of self-driving cars. We do testing of self-driving cars on private land under controlled situations. We do testing of self-driving cars on public roadways, often having to meet regulatory requirements including for example having an engineer or equivalent in the car to take over the controls if needed. And so on. Experiments big and small are needed to figure out what works and what doesn't.

Innovation

There are already some advances in AI that are allowing us to progress toward self-driving cars. We are going to need even more advances. Innovation in all aspects of technology are going to be required to achieve a true self-driving car. By no means do we already have everything in-hand that we need to get there. Expect new inventions and new approaches, new algorithms, etc.

Setbacks

Most of the pundits are avoiding talking about potential setbacks in the progress toward self-driving cars. Getting to the moon involved many setbacks, some of which you never have heard of and were buried at the time so as to not dampen enthusiasm and funding for getting to the moon. A recurring theme in many of my included essays is that there are going to be setbacks as we try to arrive at a true self-driving car. Take a deep breath and be ready. I just hope the setbacks don't completely stop progress. I am sure that it will cause progress to alter in a manner that we've not yet seen in the self-driving car field. I liken the self-driving car of today to the excitement everyone had for Uber when it first got going. Today, we have a different view of Uber and with each passing day there are more regulations to the ride sharing business and more concerns raised. The darling child only stays a darling until finally that child acts up. It will happen the same with self-driving cars.

SELF-DRIVING CARS CHALLENGES

But what exactly makes things so hard to have a true self-driving car, you might be asking. You have seen cruise control for years and years. You've lately seen cars that can do parallel parking. You've seen YouTube videos of Tesla drivers that put their hands out the window as their car zooms along the highway, and seen to therefore be in a self-driving car. Aren't we just needing to put a few more sensors onto a car and then we'll have in-hand a true self-driving car? Nope.

Consider for a moment the nature of the driving task. We don't just let anyone at any age drive a car. Worldwide, most countries won't license a driver until the age of 18, though many do allow a learner's permit at the age of 15 or 16. Some suggest that a younger age would be physically too small to reach the controls of the car. Though this might be the case, we could easily adjust the controls to allow for younger aged and thus smaller stature. It's not their physical size that matters. It's their cognitive development that matters.

To drive a car, you need to be able to reason about the car, what the car can and cannot do. You need to know how to operate the car. You need to know about how other cars on the road drive. You need to know what is allowed in driving such as speed limits and driving within marked lanes. You need to be able to react to situations and be able to avoid getting into accidents. You need to ascertain when to hit your brakes, when to steer clear of a pedestrian, and how to keep from ramming that motorcyclist that just cut you off.

Many of us had taken courses on driving. We studied about driving and took driver training. We had to take a test and pass it to be able to drive. The point being that though most adults take the driving task for granted, and we often "mindlessly" drive our cars, there is a significant amount of cognitive effort that goes into driving a car. After a while, it becomes second nature. You don't especially think about how you drive, you just do it. But, if you watch a novice driver, say a teenager learning to drive, you suddenly realize that there is a lot more complexity to it than we seem to realize.

Furthermore, driving is a very serious task. I recall when my daughter and son first learned to drive. They are both very conscientious people. They wanted to make sure that whatever they did, they did well, and that they did not harm anyone. Every day, when you get into a car, it is probably around 4,000 pounds of hefty metal and plastics (about two tons), and it is a lethal weapon. Think about it. You drive down the street in an object that weighs two tons and with the engine it can accelerate and ram into anything you want to hit. The damage a car can inflict is very scary. Both my children were surprised that they were being given the right to maneuver this monster of a beast that could cause tremendous harm entirely by merely letting go of the steering wheel for a moment or taking your eyes off the road.

In fact, in the United States alone there are about 30,000 deaths per year by auto accidents, which is around 100 per day. Given that there are about 263 million cars in the United States, I am actually more amazed that the number of fatalities is not a lot higher. During my morning commute, I look at all the thousands of cars on the freeway around me, and I think that if all of them decided to go zombie and drive in a crazy maniac way, there would be many people dead. Somehow, incredibly, each day, most people drive relatively safely. To me, that's a miracle right there. Getting millions and millions of people to be safe and sane when behind the wheel of a two ton mobile object, it's a feat that we as a society should admire with pride.

So, hopefully you are in agreement that the driving task requires a great deal of cognition. You don't' need to be especially smart to drive a car, and we've done quite a bit to make car driving viable for even the average dolt. There isn't an IQ test that you need to take to drive a car. If you can read and write, and pass a test, you pretty much can legally drive a car. There are of course some that drive a car and are not legally permitted to do so, plus there are private areas such as farms where drivers are young, but for public roadways in the United States, you can be generally of average intelligence (or less) and be able to legally drive.

This though makes it seem like the cognitive effort must not be much. If the cognitive effort was truly hard, wouldn't we only have Einstein's that could drive a car? We have made sure to keep the driving task as simple as we can, by making the controls easy and relatively standardized, and by having roads that are relatively standardized, and so on. It is as though Disneyland has put their Autopia into the real-world, by us all as a society agreeing that roads will be a certain way, and we'll all abide by the various rules of driving.

A modest cognitive task by a human is still something that stymies AI. You certainly know that AI has been able to beat chess players and be good at other kinds of games. This type of narrow cognition is not what car driving is about. Car driving is much wider. It requires knowledge about the world, which a chess playing AI system does not need to know. The cognitive aspects of driving are on the one hand seemingly simple, but at the same time require layer upon layer of knowledge about cars, people, roads, rules, and a myriad of other "common sense" aspects. We don't have any AI systems today that have that same kind of breadth and depth of awareness and knowledge.

As revealed in my essays, the self-driving car of today is using trickery to do particular tasks. It is all very narrow in operation. Plus, it currently assumes that a human driver is ready to intervene. It is like a child that we have taught to stack blocks, but we are needed to be right there in case the child stacks them too high and they begin to fall over. AI of today is brittle, it is narrow, and it does not approach the cognitive abilities of humans. This is why the true self-driving car is somewhere out in the future.

Another aspect to the driving task is that it is not solely a mind exercise. You do need to use your senses to drive. You use your eyes a vision sensors to see the road ahead. You vision capability is like a streaming video, which your brain needs to continually analyze as you drive. Where is the road? Is there a pedestrian in the way? Is there another car ahead of you? Your senses are relying a flood of info to your brain. Self-driving cars are trying to do the same, by using cameras, radar, ultrasound, and lasers. This is an attempt at mimicking how humans have senses and sensory apparatus.

Thus, the driving task is mental and physical. You use your senses, you use your arms and legs to manipulate the controls of the car, and you use your brain to assess the sensory info and direct your limbs to act upon the controls of the car. This all happens instantly. If you've ever perhaps gotten something in your eye and only had one eye available to drive with, you suddenly realize how dependent upon vision you are. If you have a broken foot with a cast, you suddenly realize how hard it is to control the brake pedal and the accelerator. If you've taken medication and your brain is maybe sluggish, you suddenly realize how much mental strain is required to drive a car.

An AI system that plays chess only needs to be focused on playing chess. The physical aspects aren't important because usually a human moves the chess pieces or the chessboard is shown on an electronic display. Using AI for a more life-and-death task such as analyzing MRI images of patients, this again does not require physical capabilities and instead is done by examining images of bits.

Driving a car is a true life-and-death task. It is a use of AI that can easily and at any moment produce death. For those colleagues of mine that are developing this AI, as am I, we need to keep in mind the somber aspects of this. We are producing software that will have in its virtual hands the lives of the occupants of the car, and the lives of those in other nearby cars, and the lives of nearby pedestrians, etc. Chess is not usually a life-or-death matter.

Driving is all around us. Cars are everywhere. Most of today's AI applications involve only a small number of people. Or, they are behind the scenes and we as humans have other recourse if the AI messes up. AI that is driving a car at 80 miles per hour on a highway had better not mess up. The consequences are grave. Multiply this by the number of cars, if we could put magically self-driving into every car in the USA, we'd have AI running in the 263 million cars. That's a lot of AI spread around. This is AI on a massive scale that we are not doing today and that offers both promise and potential peril.

There are some that want AI for self-driving cars because they envision a world without any car accidents. They envision a world in which there is no car congestion and all cars cooperate with each other. These are wonderful utopian visions.

They are also very misleading. The adoption of self-driving cars is going to be incremental and not overnight. We cannot economically just junk all existing cars. Nor are we going to be able to affordably retrofit existing cars. It is more likely that self-driving cars will be built into new cars and that over many years of gradual replacement of existing cars that we'll see the mix of self-driving cars become substantial in the real-world.

In these essays, I have tried to offer technological insights without being overly technical in my description, and also blended the business, societal, and economic aspects too. Technologists need to consider the non-technological impacts of what they do. Non-technologists should be aware of what is being developed.

We all need to work together to collectively be prepared for the enormous disruption and transformative aspects of true self-driving cars. We all need to be involved in this mother of all AI projects.

WHAT THIS BOOK PROVIDES

What does this book provide to you? It introduces many of the key elements about self-driving cars and does so with an AI based perspective. I weave together technical and non-technical aspects, readily going from being concerned about the cognitive capabilities of the driving task and how the technology is embodying this into self-driving cars, and in the next breath I discuss the societal and economic aspects.

They are all intertwined because that's the way reality is. You cannot separate out the technology per se, and instead must consider it within the milieu of what is being invented and innovated, and do so with a mindset towards the contemporary mores and culture that shape what we are doing and what we hope to do.

WHY THIS BOOK

I wrote this book to try and bring to the public view many aspects about self-driving cars that nobody seems to be discussing.

For business leaders that are either involved in making self-driving cars or that are going to leverage self-driving cars, I hope that this book will enlighten you as to the risks involved and ways in which you should be strategizing about how to deal with those risks.

For entrepreneurs, startups and other businesses that want to enter into the self-driving car market that is emerging, I hope this book sparks your interest in doing so, and provides some sense of what might be prudent to pursue.

For researchers that study self-driving cars, I hope this book spurs your interest in the risks and safety issues of self-driving cars, and also nudges you toward conducting research on those aspects.

For students in computer science or related disciplines, I hope this book will provide you with interesting and new ideas and material, for which you might conduct research or provide some career direction insights for you.

For AI companies and high-tech companies pursuing self-driving cars, this book will hopefully broaden your view beyond just the mere coding and development needed to make self-driving cars.

For all readers, I hope that you will find the material in this book to be stimulating. Some of it will be repetitive of things you already know. But I am pretty sure that you'll also find various eureka moments whereby you'll discover a new technique or approach that you had not earlier thought of. I am also betting that there will be material that forces you to rethink some of your current practices.

I am not saying you will suddenly have an epiphany and change what you are doing. I do think though that you will reconsider or perhaps revisit what you are doing.

For anyone choosing to use this book for teaching purposes, please take a look at my suggestions for doing so, as described in the Appendix. I have found the material handy in courses that I have taught, and likewise other faculty have told me that they have found the material handy, in some cases as extended readings and in other instances as a core part of their course (depending on the nature of the class).

In my writing for this book, I have tried carefully to blend both the practitioner and the academic styles of writing. It is not as dense as is typical academic journal writing, but at the same time offers depth by going into the nuances and trade-offs of various practices.

The word "deep" is in vogue today, meaning getting deeply into a subject or topic, and so is the word "unpack" which means to tease out the underlying aspects of a subject or topic. I have sought to offer material that addresses an issue or topic by going relatively deeply into it and make sure that it is well unpacked.

Finally, in any book about AI, it is difficult to use our everyday words without having some of them be misinterpreted. Specifically, it is easy to anthropomorphize AI. When I say that an AI system "knows" something, I do not want you to construe that the AI system has sentience and "knows" in the same way that humans do. They aren't that way, as yet. I have tried to use quotes around such words from time-to-time to emphasize that the words I am using should not be misinterpreted to ascribe true human intelligence to the AI systems that we know of today. If I used quotes around all such words, the book would be very difficult to read, and so I am doing so judiciously. Please keep that in mind as you read the material, thanks.

Lance B. Eliot

COMPANION BOOKS

If you find this material of interest, you might enjoy these too:

1. **"Introduction to Driverless Self-Driving Cars"** by Dr. Lance Eliot

2. **"Innovation and Thought Leadership on Self-Driving Driverless Cars"** by Dr. Lance Eliot

3. **"Advances in AI and Autonomous Vehicles: Cybernetic Self-Driving Cars"** by Dr. Lance Eliot

4. **"Self-Driving Cars: The Mother of All AI Projects"** by Dr. Lance Eliot

5. **"New Advances in AI Autonomous Driverless Self-Driving Cars"** by Dr. Lance Eliot

6. **"Autonomous Vehicle Driverless Self-Driving Cars and Artificial Intelligence"** by Dr. Lance Eliot and Michael B. Eliot

7. **"Transformative Artificial Intelligence Driverless Self-Driving Cars"** by Dr. Lance Eliot

8. **"Disruptive Artificial Intelligence and Driverless Self-Driving Cars"** by Dr. Lance Eliot

9. "State-of-the-Art AI Driverless Self-Driving Cars" by Dr. Lance Eliot

10. "Top Trends in AI Self-Driving Cars" by Dr. Lance Eliot

11. **"AI Innovations and Self-Driving Cars"** by Dr. Lance Eliot

12. **"Crucial Advances for AI Driverless Cars"** by Dr. Lance Eliot

13. **"Sociotechnical Insights and AI Driverless Cars"** by Dr. Lance Eliot.

14. **"Pioneering Advances for AI Driverless Cars"** by Dr. Lance Eliot

15. **"Leading Edge Trends for AI Driverless Cars"** by Dr. Lance Eliot

16. **"The Cutting Edge of AI Autonomous Cars"** by Dr. Lance Eliot

17. **"The Next Wave of AI Self-Driving Cars"** by Dr. Lance Eliot

18. **"Revolutionary Innovations of AI Driverless Cars"** by Dr. Lance Eliot

All of the above books are available on Amazon and at other major global booksellers.

CHAPTER 1

ELIOT FRAMEWORK FOR AI SELF-DRIVING CARS

Lance B. Eliot

CHAPTER 1

ELIOT FRAMEWORK FOR AI SELF-DRIVING CARS

This chapter is a core foundational aspect for understanding AI self-driving cars and I have used this same chapter in several of my other books to introduce the reader to essential elements of this field. Once you've read this chapter, you'll be prepared to read the rest of the material since the foundational essence of the components of autonomous AI driverless self-driving cars will have been established for you.

When I give presentations about self-driving cars and teach classes on the topic, I have found it helpful to provide a framework around which the various key elements of self-driving cars can be understood and organized (see diagram at the end of this chapter). The framework needs to be simple enough to convey the overarching elements, but at the same time not so simple that it belies the true complexity of self-driving cars. As such, I am going to describe the framework here and try to offer in a thousand words (or more!) what the framework diagram itself intends to portray.

The core elements on the diagram are numbered for ease of reference. The numbering does not suggest any kind of prioritization of the elements. Each element is crucial. Each element has a purpose, and otherwise would not be included in the framework. For some self-driving cars, a particular element might be more important or somehow distinguished in comparison to other self-driving cars.

You could even use the framework to rate a particular self-driving car, doing so by gauging how well it performs in each of the elements of the framework. I will describe each of the elements, one at a time. After doing so, I'll discuss aspects that illustrate how the elements interact and perform during the overall effort of a self-driving car.

At the Cybernetic Self-Driving Car Institute, we use the framework to keep track of what we are working on, and how we are developing software that fills in what is needed to achieve Level 5 self-driving cars.

D-01: Sensor Capture

Let's start with the one element that often gets the most attention in the press about self-driving cars, namely, the sensory devices for a self-driving car.

On the framework, the box labeled as D-01 indicates "Sensor Capture" and refers to the processes of the self-driving car that involve collecting data from the myriad of sensors that are used for a self-driving car. The types of devices typically involved are listed, such as the use of mono cameras, stereo cameras, LIDAR devices, radar systems, ultrasonic devices, GPS, IMU, and so on.

These devices are tasked with obtaining data about the status of the self-driving car and the world around it. Some of the devices are continually providing updates, while others of the devices await an indication by the self-driving car that the device is supposed to collect data. The data might be first transformed in some fashion by the device itself, or it might instead be fed directly into the sensor capture as raw data. At that point, it might be up to the sensor capture processes to do transformations on the data. This all varies depending upon the nature of the devices being used and how the devices were designed and developed.

D-02: Sensor Fusion

Imagine that your eyeballs receive visual images, your nose receives odors, your ears receive sounds, and in essence each of your distinct sensory devices is getting some form of input. The input befits the nature of the device. Likewise, for a self-driving car, the cameras provide visual images, the radar returns radar reflections, and so on.

Each device provides the data as befits what the device does.

At some point, using the analogy to humans, you need to merge together what your eyes see, what your nose smells, what your ears hear, and piece it all together into a larger sense of what the world is all about and what is happening around you. Sensor fusion is the action of taking the singular aspects from each of the devices and putting them together into a larger puzzle.

Sensor fusion is a tough task. There are some devices that might not be working at the time of the sensor capture. Or, there might some devices that are unable to report well what they have detected. Again, using a human analogy, suppose you are in a dark room and so your eyes cannot see much. At that point, you might need to rely more so on your ears and what you hear. The same is true for a self-driving car. If the cameras are obscured due to snow and sleet, it might be that the radar can provide a greater indication of what the external conditions consist of.

In the case of a self-driving car, there can be a plethora of such sensory devices. Each is reporting what it can. Each might have its difficulties. Each might have its limitations, such as how far ahead it can detect an object. All of these limitations need to be considered during the sensor fusion task.

D-03: Virtual World Model

For humans, we presumably keep in our minds a model of the world around us when we are driving a car. In your mind, you know that the car is going at say 60 miles per hour and that you are on a freeway. You have a model in your mind that your car is surrounded by other cars, and that there are lanes to the freeway. Your model is not only based on what you can see, hear, etc., but also what you know about the nature of the world. You know that at any moment that car ahead of you can smash on its brakes, or the car behind you can ram into your car, or that the truck in the next lane might swerve into your lane.

The AI of the self-driving car needs to have a virtual world model, which it then keeps updated with whatever it is receiving from the sensor fusion, which received its input from the sensor capture and the sensory devices.

D-04: System Action Plan

By having a virtual world model, the AI of the self-driving car is able to keep track of where the car is and what is happening around the car. In addition, the AI needs to determine what to do next. Should the self-driving car hit its brakes? Should the self-driving car stay in its lane or swerve into the lane to the left? Should the self-driving car accelerate or slow down?

A system action plan needs to be prepared by the AI of the self-driving car. The action plan specifies what actions should be taken. The actions need to pertain to the status of the virtual world model. Plus, the actions need to be realizable.

This realizability means that the AI cannot just assert that the self-driving car should suddenly sprout wings and fly. Instead, the AI must be bound by whatever the self-driving car can actually do, such as coming to a halt in a distance of X feet at a speed of Y miles per hour, rather than perhaps asserting that the self-driving car come to a halt in 0 feet as though it could instantaneously come to a stop while it is in motion.

D-05: Controls Activation

The system action plan is implemented by activating the controls of the car to act according to what the plan stipulates. This might mean that the accelerator control is commanded to increase the speed of the car. Or, the steering control is commanded to turn the steering wheel 30 degrees to the left or right.

One question arises as to whether or not the controls respond as they are commanded to do. In other words, suppose the AI has commanded the accelerator to increase, but for some reason it does not do so. Or, maybe it tries to do so, but the speed of the car does not increase. The controls activation feeds back into the virtual world model, and simultaneously the virtual world model is getting updated from the sensors, the sensor capture, and the sensor fusion. This allows the AI to ascertain what has taken place as a result of the controls being commanded to take some kind of action.

By the way, please keep in mind that though the diagram seems to have a linear progression to it, the reality is that these are all aspects of the self-driving car that are happening in parallel and simultaneously. The sensors are capturing data, meanwhile the sensor fusion is taking place, meanwhile the virtual model is being updated, meanwhile the system action plan is being formulated and reformulated, meanwhile the controls are being activated.

This is the same as a human being that is driving a car. They are eyeballing the road, meanwhile they are fusing in their mind the sights, sounds, etc., meanwhile their mind is updating their model of the world around them, meanwhile they are formulating an action plan of what to do, and meanwhile they are pushing their foot onto the pedals and steering the car. In the normal course of driving a car, you are doing all of these at once. I mention this so that when you look at the diagram, you will think of the boxes as processes that are all happening at the same time, and not as though only one happens and then the next.

They are shown diagrammatically in a simplistic manner to help comprehend what is taking place. You though should also realize that they are working in parallel and simultaneous with each other. This is a tough aspect in that the inter-element communications involve latency and other aspects that must be taken into account. There can be delays in one element updating and then sharing its latest status with other elements.

D-06: Automobile & CAN

Contemporary cars use various automotive electronics and a Controller Area Network (CAN) to serve as the components that underlie the driving aspects of a car. There are Electronic Control Units (ECU's) which control subsystems of the car, such as the engine, the brakes, the doors, the windows, and so on.

The elements D-01, D-02, D-03, D-04, D-05 are layered on top of the D-06, and must be aware of the nature of what the D-06 is able to do and not do.

D-07: In-Car Commands

Humans are going to be occupants in self-driving cars. In a Level 5 self-driving car, there must be some form of communication that takes place between the humans and the self-driving car. For example, I go into a self-driving car and tell it that I want to be driven over to Disneyland, and along the way I want to stop at In-and-Out Burger. The self-driving car now parses what I've said and tries to then establish a means to carry out my wishes.

In-car commands can happen at any time during a driving journey. Though my example was about an in-car command when I first got into my self-driving car, it could be that while the self-driving car is carrying out the journey that I change my mind. Perhaps after getting stuck in traffic, I tell the self-driving car to forget about getting the burgers and just head straight over to the theme park. The self-driving car needs to be alert to in-car commands throughout the journey.

D-08: V2X Communications

We will ultimately have self-driving cars communicating with each other, doing so via V2V (Vehicle-to-Vehicle) communications. We will also have self-driving cars that communicate with the roadways and other aspects of the transportation infrastructure, doing so via V2I (Vehicle-to-Infrastructure).

The variety of ways in which a self-driving car will be communicating with other cars and infrastructure is being called V2X, whereby the letter X means whatever else we identify as something that a car should or would want to communicate with. The V2X communications will be taking place simultaneous with everything else on the diagram, and those other elements will need to incorporate whatever it gleans from those V2X communications.

D-09: Deep Learning

The use of Deep Learning permeates all other aspects of the self-driving car. The AI of the self-driving car will be using deep learning to do a better job at the systems action plan, and at the controls activation, and at the sensor fusion, and so on.

Currently, the use of artificial neural networks is the most prevalent form of deep learning. Based on large swaths of data, the neural networks attempt to "learn" from the data and therefore direct the efforts of the self-driving car accordingly.

D-10: Tactical AI

Tactical AI is the element of dealing with the moment-to-moment driving of the self-driving car. Is the self-driving car staying in its lane of the freeway? Is the car responding appropriately to the controls commands? Are the sensory devices working?

For human drivers, the tactical equivalent can be seen when you watch a novice driver such as a teenager that is first driving. They are focused on the mechanics of the driving task, keeping their eye on the road while also trying to properly control the car.

D-11: Strategic AI

The Strategic AI aspects of a self-driving car are dealing with the larger picture of what the self-driving car is trying to do. If I had asked that the self-driving car take me to Disneyland, there is an overall journey map that needs to be kept and maintained.

There is an interaction between the Strategic AI and the Tactical AI. The Strategic AI is wanting to keep on the mission of the driving, while the Tactical AI is focused on the particulars underway in the driving effort. If the Tactical AI seems to wander away from the overarching mission, the Strategic AI wants to see why and get things back on track. If the Tactical AI realizes that there is something amiss on the self-driving car, it needs to alert the Strategic AI accordingly and have an adjustment to the overarching mission that is underway.

D-12: Self-Aware AI

Very few of the self-driving cars being developed are including a Self-Aware AI element, which we at the Cybernetic Self-Driving Car Institute believe is crucial to Level 5 self-driving cars.

The Self-Aware AI element is intended to watch over itself, in the sense that the AI is making sure that the AI is working as intended. Suppose you had a human driving a car, and they were starting to drive erratically. Hopefully, their own self-awareness would make them realize they themselves are driving poorly, such as perhaps starting to fall asleep after having been driving for hours on end. If you had a passenger in the car, they might be able to alert the driver if the driver is starting to do something amiss. This is exactly what the Self-Aware

AI element tries to do, it becomes the overseer of the AI, and tries to detect when the AI has become faulty or confused, and then find ways to overcome the issue.

D-13: Economic

The economic aspects of a self-driving car are not per se a technology aspect of a self-driving car, but the economics do indeed impact the nature of a self-driving car. For example, the cost of outfitting a self-driving car with every kind of possible sensory device is prohibitive, and so choices need to be made about which devices are used. And, for those sensory devices chosen, whether they would have a full set of features or a more limited set of features.

We are going to have self-driving cars that are at the low-end of a consumer cost point, and others at the high-end of a consumer cost point. You cannot expect that the self-driving car at the low-end is going to be as robust as the one at the high-end. I realize that many of the self-driving car pundits are acting as though all self-driving cars will be the same, but they won't be. Just like anything else, we are going to have self-driving cars that have a range of capabilities. Some will be better than others. Some will be safer than others. This is the way of the real-world, and so we need to be thinking about the economics aspects when considering the nature of self-driving cars.

D-14: Societal

This component encompasses the societal aspects of AI which also impacts the technology of self-driving cars. For example, the famous Trolley Problem involves what choices should a self-driving car make when faced with life-and-death matters. If the self-driving car is about to either hit a child standing in the roadway, or instead ram into a tree at the side of the road and possibly kill the humans in the self-driving car, which choice should be made?

We need to keep in mind the societal aspects will underlie the AI of the self-driving car. Whether we are aware of it explicitly or not, the AI will have embedded into it various societal assumptions.

D-15: Innovation

I included the notion of innovation into the framework because we can anticipate that whatever a self-driving car consists of, it will continue to be innovated over time. The self-driving cars coming out in the next several years will undoubtedly be different and less innovative than the versions that come out in ten years hence, and so on.

Framework Overall

For those of you that want to learn about self-driving cars, you can potentially pick a particular element and become specialized in that aspect. Some engineers are focusing on the sensory devices. Some engineers focus on the controls activation. And so on. There are specialties in each of the elements.

Researchers are likewise specializing in various aspects. For example, there are researchers that are using Deep Learning to see how best it can be used for sensor fusion. There are other researchers that are using Deep Learning to derive good System Action Plans. Some are studying how to develop AI for the Strategic aspects of the driving task, while others are focused on the Tactical aspects.

A well-prepared all-around software developer that is involved in self-driving cars should be familiar with all of the elements, at least to the degree that they know what each element does. This is important since whatever piece of the pie that the software developer works on, they need to be knowledgeable about what the other elements are doing.

Lance B. Eliot

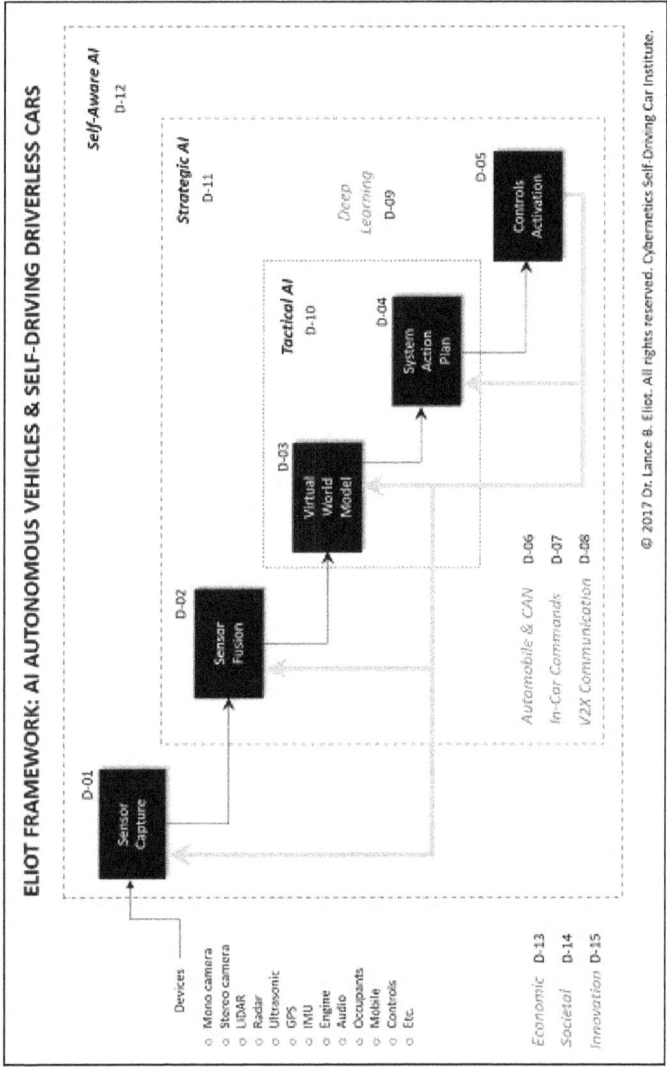

ELIOT FRAMEWORK: AI AUTONOMOUS VEHICLES & SELF-DRIVING DRIVERLESS CARS

Self-Aware AI
D-12

Strategic AI
D-11

Deep Learning
D-09

Tactical AI
D-10

Sensor Capture
D-01

Sensor Fusion
D-02

Virtual World Model
D-03

System Action Plan
D-04

Controls Activation
D-05

Devices
o Mono camera
o Stereo camera
o LIDAR
o Radar
o Ultrasonic
o GPS
o IMU
o Engine
o Audio
o Occupants
o Mobile
o Controls
o Etc.

Automobile & CAN   D-06
In-Car Commands   D-07
V2X Communication   D-08

Economic   D-13
Societal   D-14
Innovation D-15

Lance B. Eliot

CHAPTER 2

EXASCALE SUPERCOMPUTERS AND AI SELF-DRIVING CARS

Lance B. Eliot

CHAPTER 2

EXASCALE SUPERCOMPUTERS AND AI SELF-DRIVING CARS

Supercomputers are great.

If you are really into computing and computers, you've got to admire and be fascinated by supercomputing. It is similar to really being into cars and keeping in tune with the fastest sports cars and pushing the limits on technology of one kind or another. Just as most of us cannot afford those high-priced souped-up roadsters that cost a big wad of cash, same too can be said about supercomputers. The only players in supercomputers are those that can plunk down tons of dough (well, at least for those that own supercomputers, such as huge companies or national agencies; I'll say more about using rather than buying them, later-on herein).

One of my favorite supercomputers was the Cray-1. It was brought to the world by computer inventor extraordinaire Seymour Cray in the mid-1970s and ran at an astounding 200 MFLOPS (M is for Mega, FLOPS is for floating point operations per second). This was super-fast at the time. There was a popular insider joke at the time. The joke was that the Cray-1 was so fast that it could complete an infinite loop in less than one second.

For those of you that haven't fallen to the floor in laughter, the joke is that an infinite loop presumably would never end and so the Cray-1 was so tremendously fast that it could even finish an infinite loop. Ha!

31

By the way, you can pretty much use that joke still today and just mention the name of a more contemporary supercomputer (you'll be the life of any nerd party).

The current reining champ of supercomputers is the Summit supercomputer at Oak Ridge National Labs (ORNL). In June of this year, the Summit was crowned the fastest supercomputer and placed at the top of the classic and ever-popular Top500 list (this is a listing of the top supercomputers ranked by speed and it is fun to keep tabs to see who makes the list and what their rank is). Similar to chess masters and their rankings, anyone into supercomputers knows at least who the top 10 are on the Top500 list and likely has familiarity with at least the top 30 or so.

Summit is rated at about 122.3 PFLOPS (P is for Peta, which is 1,000 million million). In theory, if Summit could just go all out and run at a maximum raw speed, it presumably could do about 200 PFLOPS. As they say, we've come a long way, baby – meaning that if you compare the Cray-1 at 200 MFLOPS versus today's Summit at 200 PFLOPS, the speed difference is like night versus day.

It is said that to be able to do as many calculations per second as can Summit, every person on Earth would need to be able to perform around 16 million calculations per second. Why don't we try that? Let's get everyone to stop what they are doing right now, and perform 16 million calculations, doing so in one second of time. Might be challenging.

Maybe one way to think of the vast growth in speed from the Cray-1 days to the Summit involves considering space rather than time, in terms of if you had something that could store data on the basis of megabytes you might be able to keep a few written novels in that amount of space, while in comparison for petabytes you could keep perhaps all of the data contained in the United States libraries (please note that's a rough approximation and only intended to suggest the magnitude difference).

Let's consider the prefixes used and the amounts involved:

Mega = $10 \verb|^| 6$
Giga = $10 \verb|^| 9$
Tera = $10 \verb|^| 12$
Peta = $10 \verb|^| 15$
Exa = $10 \verb|^| 18$

I'm using the symbol ""^"" to mean "to the power of" and for example the Mega is 1 x 10 to the 6th power, while Giga is 1 x 10 to the 9th power, and so on.

Having the fastest supercomputer is considered at times an indicator of who is "winning" the race in terms of advancing computers and computing.

Right now, the United States holds the top slot with Summit, but for the last several years it was China with their Sunway TaihuLight supercomputer. How long will the United States hang onto the Number 1 position in supercomputers? Hard to say. The official Top500 list is updated twice per year. You've got the United States, China, Europe, Japan, and other big players all vying to get onto the list and get to the very top of the list. Some predict that Japan's Post-K might make the top in 2020, and the United States might reclaim the title in 2021, though China might move back into the top slot during those time frames too (it can be hard to predict because the big players are all in the midst of developing newer and faster supercomputers but the end-date of when they will be finished is often hazy or not revealed).

Is it fair to say that whichever country makes or has the fastest supercomputer is leading the race towards advancing computers? Probably not, but it is an easy way to play that game and one that many seem to believe merits attention (note that the Summit was developed at an estimated cost of around $200 million, which per my point earlier emphasizes that you need a big wallet to make one of these supercomputers).

To benchmark the speed, it is customary to have supercomputers run the famous LINPACK benchmark software. LINPACK was originally a set of Fortran program routines for doing various kinds of algebraic mathematics and it eventually became associated with being a benchmark for computer speed (today you might use LAPACK in lieu of LINPACK, if you are in need of a set of routines for algebraic related aspects). The handiness of the LINPACK benchmark is that it involves the computer doing a "pure calculation" kind of problem by trying to solve a system of linear equations. In that sense, it is essentially restricted to the use of straight-ahead floating-point operations and akin to perhaps having a horse run flat-out on a track as fast as it can.

Some criticize the use of such a benchmark as somewhat off-kilter because supercomputers are likely going to be doing more than relatively simplistic mathematical calculations. Such critics say that it distorts the design of the supercomputer by having the supercomputer makers aim to do maximum FLOPS and not necessarily be able to do other kinds of computer-related tasks very well.

Like it or not, the world has seemed to agree to the LINPACK benchmark, actually, more formally usually the HPL (High Performance LINPACK) which is optimized more so for this kind of benchmarking. It would be hard to get everyone to switch to some other benchmark and also would make it difficult to make comparisons to previous rankings. This same kind of argument happens in sports such as proposals to change some of the rules of football or baseball, and in so doing it can make prior records become no longer relevant and readily usable.

One concern that some raise is the vast amount of electrical power often consumed by these supercomputers. The amount of electrical power usage is often expressed in FLOPS per watt (the Summit is about 13.889 GFLOPS per watt). Some believe that the proper ranking of supercomputers should be a combination of the raw speed metric of supercomputers by the electrical power consumption metric, which then would perhaps force the supercomputer designers to be more prudent about how much electrical power is being used. Instead, there are really two lists, the raw speed list and the other list is the electrical power efficiency list. The glory tends to go toward the raw speed list.

This indication about electrical power consumption brings up another significant point, namely that the cost to run a supercomputer is about as astronomical as is the outright price of the supercomputer.

Besides the need for lots of electricity, another noteworthy factor in supercomputer design involves the heat that can build-up in the supercomputer. With lots of fast processors comes the generation of heat. The closer you try to put these processors to each other, the more heat that you have in a tightened area. You want to put the processors as close as possible to each other so as to minimize the delay times of the processors communicating with each other (the more the distance between the processors, the longer the latency times).

So, if you are packing together thousands of processors, doing so to add speed and reduce latency, you also tend to get high heat density. Life is always one kind of a trade-off versus another. One of the most popular cooling methods for supercomputers involves using liquid cooling. It might seem odd to consider putting liquid (of any kind) anywhere near the electrically running processors, but you can nonetheless have tubes of liquid to help bring coolness to the processors and aid in dissipating heat from them. Air cooling is also possible.

The Cray-1 was known for its unusual shape, consisting of a main tower that was curved like the letter "C" and had a concentric bench around it. It was described at the time as the world's most costly loveseat due to the unique physical design. Looking at it from above, you could see that it had the shape of the letter "C" and was said to be designed in that manner to reduce the distance between the processors and aid the use of the Freon cooling system (note that it was also suggested that Cray liked the notion of his supercomputer spelling out the letter of his last name!). If you'd like to see and touch one of the original Cray-1's you can do so at the Computer History Museum in Mountain View, California.

Here's a question for you. Which would you prefer to do, have your supercomputer uses lots and lots of off-the-shelf processors or have it contain lots of specialized processors made specifically for the supercomputer?

That's a big design question for any supercomputer. Using processors that already exist is certainly easier because you don't need to design and build new processors. Instead, your focus becomes how to best hook them up with each other. But, you are also then stuck with however good (or bad) those processors are in terms of speed of their individual performance. As Seymour Cray had remarked back in the days of the early arguments about whether to use off-the-shelf versus specialized processors (he favored specialized processors), he oft would say that if he was trying to plow a field, he'd rather use 2 oxen in lieu of using 1,024 chickens.

A slight twist on which processors to use has emerged due to the advent of Graphical Processing Units (GPU's). GPU's were originally developed as processors intended to be dedicated to tasks involving graphics display and transformations. They kept getting pushed to be faster and faster to keep up with the evolving desire for clean and fully streaming graphics. Eventually, it was realized that you could make a General Purpose GPU (GPGPU), and consider using those unconventional non-traditional processors as the basis for your supercomputer.

Some though say that you ought to go with the stripped-down bare bones kind of processors that can be optimized for pure FLOPS kind of speed. Reduced Instruction Set Computing (RISC) processors arose to take us back to a time when the processor wasn't overly complex and you could optimize it to do some fundamental things like maximize FLOPS. Perhaps one of the most notable such trends was indicated by the Scalable Processor Architecture (SPARC) that was promulgated by the computer vendor Sun.

Often referred to as High Performance Computing (HPC), supercomputers exploit parallelism to gain their superfast speeds. Massively Parallel Processing (MPP) consists of having a massive number of processors that can work in parallel. One of the great challenges of truly leveraging the parallelism involves whether or not whatever you are computing with your MPP can be divided up into pieces to sufficiently make use of the parallel capability.

If I go to the store to go shopping and have a list of items to buy, I can only go so fast throughout the store to do my shopping. I might optimize my path to make sure that I get each item in a sequence that reduces how far I need to walk throughout the store. Nonetheless, I'm only one person, I believe, and thus there's only so much I can do to speed-up my shopping effort.

On the other hand, if I added an additional person, we potentially could speed-up the shopping. We could possibly shop in parallel. Suppose though that I had only one copy of the shopping list and we both had to walk around the store together while shopping. Probably not much of a speed-up. If I could divide the shopping list into two parts, giving half to the other person and my keeping half, we now might have a good chance of speeding things up.

If I am not thoughtful about how I divide up the list of shopping items, it could be that the speed-up won't be much. I need to consider a sensible way to leverage the parallelism. Imagine too if I got three more people to help with the shopping. I'd want to find a means to further subdivide the master list in a sensible manner that tries to gain as much speed-up as feasible via the parallelism.

As such, suppose that you've got yourself a supercomputer like the Summit, and it contains over 9,000 22-core CPU's (IBM Power9's) and another 27,000+ GPU's (NVIDIA Tesla V100's). It takes up an area about the size of two tennis courts, and it uses about 4,000 gallons of water per minute to cool it.

You decide to have it play tic-tac-toe with you.

It would seem doubtful that you would need this kind of impressive "hunk of iron" that the Summit has, in order to play you in such a simple game. How many processors would you need to use for your tic-tac-toe? Let's say you devote a handful to this task, which is more than enough. Meanwhile, the other processors are sitting around with nothing to do. All those unused processors, all that used up space, all that cost, all that cooling, and most of the supercomputer is just whistling Dixie while you are playing it in tic-tac-toe.

The point being that there's not much value in having a supercomputer that is superfast due to exploiting parallelism if you are unable to have a problem that can lend itself to utilizing the parallel architecture. You can essentially render a superfast computer into being a do-little supercomputer by trying to mismatch it with something that won't scale-up and use the parallelism.

What kind of uses can a supercomputer be sensibly put to? The most common uses include doing large-scale climate modeling, weather modeling, oil and gas exploration analysis, genetics analysis, etc. Each of those kinds of problems can be expressed into a mathematical format and can be divided up into parallel efforts.

Sometimes such tasks are considered to be "embarrassingly parallel," which means that they are ready-made for parallelism and you don't need to go to a lot of work to figure out how to turn the task into something that uses parallelism. I am not trivializing the effort involved in programming these tasks to use the parallelism and only suggesting that sometimes the task presents itself in a manner that won't require unimaginable ways of getting to a parallel approach. If you don't like the use of the word "embarrassingly" then you can substitute it with the word "pleasingly" (as in "pleasingly parallel" meaning the task fits well to being parallelized).

Whether you use RISC or GPGPU's or anything conventional as your core processor, there are some critics of this "traditionalist" approach to supercomputers that say we've got to pursue the whole supercomputer topic in an entirely different way. They ask a simple question – do humans think by using FLOPS? Though we don't yet really know how the human brain works, I think it is relatively fair to assert that humans probably do not use FLOPS in their minds.

For those of us in the AI field, we generally tend to believe that aiming at neurons is a better shot at ultimately trying to have a computer that can do what the human brain can do. Sure, you can simulate a neuron with a FLOPS mode conventional processor, but do we really believe that simulating a neuron in that manner will get us to the same level as a human brain? Many of the Machine Learning (ML) and Artificial Neural Network (ANN) advocates would say no.

Instead, it is thought that we need to have specialized processors that act more like neurons. Note that they are still not the same as neurons, and you can argue that they are once again just a simulation of a neuron, though the counter-argument is yes that's true, but they are closer to being like a neuron than conventional processors are. You are welcome to go back-and-forth on that argument for about five minutes, if you wish to do so, and then continue ahead herein.

These neuron inspired supercomputers are typically referred to as neuromorphic supercomputers.

Some exciting news occurred recently when the University of Manchester announced that their neuromorphic supercomputer now has 1 million processors. This system uses the Spiking Neural Network Architecture known as SpiNNaker. They were able to put together a model that contained about 80,000 "neurons" and had around 300 million "synapses" (I am putting quotes around the words neuron and synapse because I don't want to conflate the real biological wetware with the much less equivalent computer simulated versions).

It is quite exciting to see these kinds of advances are occurring in neuromorphic supercomputers and it bodes well for what might be coming down the pike. The hope is to aim for a model with 1 billion "neurons" in it.

Just to let you know, and I am not trying to be a party pooper on this, but the human brain is estimated to have perhaps 100 billion neurons and maybe 1 quadrillion synapses. Even once we can get a 1 billion "neurons" supercomputer going, it will still only represent perhaps 1% of the total number of neurons in a person's head. Some believe that until we are able to reach nearer to the 100 billion mark that we will not be able to do much with the lesser number of simulated neurons. Perhaps you need a certain preponderance of mass of neurons before intelligence can emerge.

Though we might not be able to approach soon the simulations needed for "recreating" human-like minds, we can at least perhaps do some nifty explorations involving other kinds of creatures.

A lobster has about 100,000 neurons, while a honey bee has about 960,000, and a frog around 16,000,000. A mouse has around 71,000,000 neurons and a rat about 148,000,000. A dog has around 2 billion neurons, while a chimpanzee has about 28 billion. Hopefully, we can begin to do some interesting explorations of how the brain works via neuromorphic computing for these creatures. But, be forewarned, using only the count of neurons is a bit misleading and there's a lot more involved in getting toward "intelligence" that exists in the minds of any such animals.

There's another camp or tribe in the processors design debate that argues we need to completely rethink the topic and pursue quantum computers instead of the other ways of approaching the matter.

If we can really get quantum superposition and entanglement to work to our bidding (key structural elements of quantum computers, which are only being done in research labs and experimentally right now), it does appear that some incredible speed-up's can be had in terms of "classical" computing. The quantum advocates are aiming to achieve "quantum supremacy" over various aspects of classical computing. For now, it's worthwhile to keep in mind that Albert Einstein had said that quantum entanglement was spooky and so the race to create a true quantum computer might bring us closer to understanding mysteries of the universe such as the nature of matter, space, and time, if we can get practical quantum computers to be achieved.

In terms of conventional supercomputers, the race currently is about trying to get beyond petaflops and reach the exalted exaflops.

An exaFLOPS is the equivalent of 1,000 petaFLOPS. I had mentioned earlier that Summit can top off at 200 petaFLOPS, but through some clever tricks they were able to apparently achieve 1.88 exaFLOPS performance for a certain kind of genomes problem and reach 3.3 exaFLOPS for certain kinds of mixed precision calculations. This is not quite a true unvarnished onset of exaFLOPS and so the world is still waiting for a supercomputer that can reach the exaFLOPS in a more sustainable traditionalist conventional sense.

I think you ought to get a bumper sticker for your car that says exascale supercomputers are almost here. Maybe by 2020 or 2021 you'll be able to change the bumper sticker and say that exascale computing has arrived.

Speaking of cars, you might be wondering what does this have to do with AI self-driving cars?

At the Cybernetic AI Self-Driving Car Institute, we are developing AI software for self-driving cars. Supercomputers can be a big help toward the advent of AI self-driving cars.

Allow me to elaborate.

I'd like to first clarify and introduce the notion that there are varying levels of AI self-driving cars. The topmost level is considered Level 5. A Level 5 self-driving car is one that is being driven by the AI and there is no human driver involved. For the design of Level 5 self-driving cars, the auto makers are even removing the gas pedal, brake pedal, and steering wheel, since those are contraptions used by human drivers. The Level 5 self-driving car is not being driven by a human and nor is there an expectation that a human driver will be present in the self-driving car. It's all on the shoulders of the AI to drive the car.

For self-driving cars less than a Level 5, there must be a human driver present in the car. The human driver is currently considered the responsible party for the acts of the car. The AI and the human driver are co-sharing the driving task. In spite of this co-sharing, the human is supposed to remain fully immersed into the driving task and be ready at all times to perform the driving task. I've repeatedly warned about the dangers of this co-sharing arrangement and predicted it will produce many untoward results.

Let's focus herein on the true Level 5 self-driving car. Much of the comments apply to the less than Level 5 self-driving cars too, but the fully autonomous AI self-driving car will receive the most attention in this discussion.

Here's the usual steps involved in the AI driving task:

- Sensor data collection and interpretation
- Sensor fusion
- Virtual world model updating
- AI action planning
- Car controls command issuance

Another key aspect of AI self-driving cars is that they will be driving on our roadways in the midst of human driven cars too. There are some pundits of AI self-driving cars that continually refer to a utopian world in which there are only AI self-driving cars on the public roads. Currently there are about 250+ million conventional cars in the United States alone, and those cars are not going to magically disappear or become true Level 5 AI self-driving cars overnight.

Indeed, the use of human driven cars will last for many years, likely many decades, and the advent of AI self-driving cars will occur while there are still human driven cars on the roads. This is a crucial point since this means that the AI of self-driving cars needs to be able to contend with not just other AI self-driving cars, but also contend with human driven cars.

It is easy to envision a simplistic and rather unrealistic world in which all AI self-driving cars are politely interacting with each other and being civil about roadway interactions. That's not what is going to be happening for the foreseeable future. AI self-driving cars and human driven cars will need to be able to cope with each other.

Returning to the topic of supercomputers, let's consider how today's supercomputers and tomorrow's even faster supercomputers can be advantageous to AI self-driving cars.

Suppose you were an auto maker or tech firm that had access to an exascale supercomputer. You have $10 \char94 18$ exaFLOPS available to do whatever you want with those enormous processing cycles.

First, you can pretty much cross off the list of possibilities the notion that you would put the exascale supercomputer on-board of an AI self-driving car. Unless the self-driving car is the size of about two football fields and has a nuclear power plant included, you are not going to get the exascale supercomputer to fit into the self-driving car. Perhaps some decades from now the continued progress on miniaturization might allow the exascale supercomputer to get small enough to fit into a self-driving car, which I say now so that decades from today no one can look back and quote me as suggesting it could never happen (just like those old predictions that mainframe computers would never be the size of PCs, yet that's somewhat what we have today).

As an aside, even though the exascale supercomputer won't fit into a self-driving car, there are a lot of software related techniques that can be gleaned from supercomputing and be used for AI self-driving cars. One big plus about supercomputing is that it tends to push forward on new advances for operating systems (typically a Linux-derivative), and for databases, and for networking, and so on. That's actually another reason to want to have supercomputers, namely that it usually brings forth other kinds of breakthroughs, either software related ones or hardware related ones.

In any case, throw in the towel about getting a supercomputer to fit into an AI self-driving car. Then what?

Let's consider how a supercomputer and an AI self-driving car might try to work with each other. Keep in mind that there is only so much computing processing capability that we can pack into an AI self-driving car. The more processors we jam into the self-driving car, the more it uses up space for passengers, and the more it uses up electrical power, and the more heat it generates, and importantly the costlier the AI self-driving car is going to become.

Thus, the aim is the Goldilocks approach, having just the right amount of processing capability loaded into the AI self-driving car. Not too little, and not too much.

It would be handy to have an arrangement whereby if the AI self-driving car needed some more processing capability that it could magically suddenly have it available. Via the OTA (Over-The-Air) capability of an AI self-driving car, you might be able to tap into a supercomputer that's accessed through the cloud of the auto maker or tech firm that made the AI system.

The OTA is usually intended to allow for an AI self-driving car to upload data, such as the data being collected via its multitude of sensors. The cloud of the auto maker or tech firm can then analyze the data and try to find patterns that might be interesting, new, and useful. The OTA can also be used to download into the AI self-driving car the latest software updates, patches, and other aspects that the auto maker or tech firm wants to be on-board of the self-driving car.

Normally, the OTA is generally considered a "batch oriented" kind of activity. A batch of data is stored on-board the self-driving car and when the self-driving car is in a posture that it can do a heavy sized upload, it does so (such as parked in your garage at home, charging up, and having access to your home high-speed WiFi, or maybe doing so at your office at work). Likewise, the downloads to the AI self-driving car tend to take place when the self-driving car is not otherwise active, making things a bit safer since you would not want an in-motion AI self-driving car on the freeway to suddenly get an updated patch and maybe either be distracted or get confused by the hasty change.

Of course, a supercomputer could be sitting there in the cloud and be used for aiding the behind-the-scenes aspects of analyzing the data and helping to prepare downloads. In that sense, the AI self-driving car has no real-time "connection" or collaboration with the supercomputer. The supercomputer is beyond the direct reach of the AI self-driving car.

Suppose though that we opted to have the supercomputer act as a kind of reserve of added computational capability for the AI self-driving car? Whenever the AI self-driving car needs to ramp-up and process something, it could potentially seek to find out if the exascale supercomputer could help out. If there is a connection feasible and the supercomputer is available, the AI self-driving car might provide the supercomputer with processing tasks and then see what the supercomputer has to report back about it.

Imagine that the AI self-driving car has been driving along on a street it has never been on before. Using somewhat rudimentary navigation, it successfully makes its way along the street. Meanwhile, it is collecting lots of data about the street scene, including video and pictures, radar images, LIDAR, and the like. The AI self-driving car pumps this up to the cloud, and asks the supercomputer to rapidly analyze it.

Doing a full analysis by the on-board processors of the self-driving car would take a while to do, simply because those processors are much slower than the supercomputer. Furthermore, the on-board processors are doing already a lot of work trying to navigate down the street without hitting anything. It would be handy to push over to the supercomputer the data and see what it can find, perhaps being able to do so more quickly than the AI self-driving car.

The speed aspects of the supercomputer allow a deeper analysis too than what the on-board processors could likely do in the same amount of time. It is like a chess match. In chess, you try to consider your next move and the move of your opponent in response to your move. If the chess clock allows enough time, you should also be considering how you will move after your opponent has moved, and then your next move, and so on. These are called ply and you want to try and look ahead as many ply as you can. But, given constraints on time, chess players often can only consider a few ply ahead, plus it can be mentally arduous to go much further ahead in contemplating next moves.

The AI on-board the self-driving car might be doing a single ply of analyzing the street scene, meanwhile it provides the street scene data to the supercomputer via the cloud and asks it to simultaneously do an analysis. The supercomputer might then let the AI on-board the self-driving car know that ahead of it is a tree that might be ready to fall onto the road. The AI on-board had only recognized that a tree existed at that location but had not been able to do any kind of analysis further about it. The supercomputer did a deeper analysis and was able to discern that based on the type of tree, the angle of the tree, and other factors, there is a high chance of it falling over. This would be handy for the AI on-board the self-driving car to be aware of and be wary of going near the tree.

Notice that the AI on-board did not necessarily need the use of the supercomputer per se. The AI was able to independently navigate the street. The supercomputer was considered an auxiliary capability. If the supercomputer was available and could be reached, great. But, if the supercomputer was not available or could not be reached, the AI was still sufficient on-board to do whatever the driving task consisted of.

The approach of having the AI on-board the self-driving car make use of a supercomputer in the cloud would not be so straightforward as it might seem.

The AI self-driving car has to be able to have an electronic communications connection viable enough to do so. This can be tricky when an AI self-driving car is in-motion, perhaps moving at 80 miles per hour down a freeway. Plus, if the AI self-driving car is in a remote location such as a highway that cuts across a state, there might not be much Internet access available.

It is hoped that the advent of 5G as a WiFi standard will allow for improved electronic communications, including speed and being available in more places than traditional WiFi.

The electronic connection might be subject to disruption and therefore the AI self-driving car has to be wary of requiring that the supercomputer respond. If the AI is dependent entirely on the supercomputer to make crucial real-time decisions, this would most likely be a recipe for failure (such as crashing into a wall or otherwise making a bad move). That's why I earlier phrased it as a collaborative kind of relationship between the AI on-board and the supercomputer, including that the supercomputer is considered an auxiliary ally. If the auxiliary ally is not reachable, the AI on-board has to continue along on its own.

Another somewhat similar approach could be the use of edge computing to be an auxiliary ally of the AI on-board the self-driving car. Edge computing refers to having computer processing capabilities closer to the "edge" of wherever they are needed. Some have suggested that we ought to be place computer processing capabilities at the side of our roads and highways. An AI self-driving car could then tap into that added processing capability. This would be faster and presumably more reliable since the computing is sitting right there next to the road, versus a supercomputer that's half-way around the world and being accessed via a cloud.

We might then opt to have both edge computing and the exascale supercomputer. The AI on-board the self-driving car might first try to tap into the edge computing nearby. The edge computing would then try to tap into the supercomputer. They all work together in a federated manner. The supercomputer might then do some work for the AI on-board that has been handed to it via the edge computing. The edge computing remains in-touch with the AI on-bard the self-driving car as it zooms down the highway. The supercomputer responds to give its results to the edge computing, which in turn hands it over to the AI self-driving car.

This arrangement might also relieve the AI self-driving car from having to deal with any vagaries or issues that arise between the edge computers and the supercomputer in the cloud. It is all hidden away from the AI on-board the self-driving car. This allows the on-board AI to continue focusing on the driving task.

I'm sure you can imagine how convoluted this can potentially become. If the AI on-board has opted to make use of the edge computing and the supercomputer, or even just the supercomputer, how long should it wait before deciding that things aren't going to happen soon enough. Driving down a street and waiting to get back the analysis of the supercomputer, time is ticking, and the AI on-board has to be presumably keeping the car moving along. It's conceivable that the analysis about the street scene and the potential fall-over tree wouldn't be provided by the supercomputer until after the AI has already finished driving down the entire block.

A delayed response doesn't though mean that the supercomputer processing was necessarily wasted. It could be that the AI self-driving car is going to drive back along that same street again, maybe on the way back out of town. Knowing about the potentially falling tree is still handy.

This brings us to another whole facet about the supercomputer aspects. So far, I've been focusing on a single self-driving car and its AI. The auto maker or tech firm that made the AI self-driving car would consider that they have an entire fleet of self-driving cars. For example, when providing a patch or other update, the auto maker or tech firm would use the cloud to push down via OTA the update to presumably all of the AI self-driving cars that they've sold or otherwise have on the roadways (that's their fleet of cars).

If the supercomputer figured out that the tree might be ready to fall, it could update the entire fleet with that indication, posting something about the tree into the mapping portion of their on-board systems. It would not have to do this for all self-driving cars in the fleet and perhaps choose just those self-driving cars that might be nearby to the street that has the potentially falling tree.

Overall, the supercomputer could be aiding the ongoing Machine Learning aspects of the AI self-driving cars. Trying to get the processors on-board a self-driving car to do much Machine Learning is a likely exercise in futility because those processors aren't either powerful enough or they are preoccupied (rightfully) with the driving tasks of the self-driving car. Some believe that self-driving cars will be running non-stop around the clock, as such, there might not be much idle or extra time available for the processors on-board to be tackling Machine Learning kinds of enhancements to the AI on-board.

Besides using a supercomputer to aid in the real-time or near real-time aspects of an AI self-driving car, there is also the potential to use the supercomputer for performing simulations that are pertinent to AI self-driving cars.

Before an AI self-driving car gets onto an actual roadway, hopefully the auto maker or tech firm has done a somewhat extensive and exhaustive number of simulations to try and ferret out whether the AI is really ready for driving on our public roads. These simulations can be rather complex if you want them to be as realistic as possible. The amount of processing required to do the simulations can be quite high and using a supercomputer would certainly be handy.

Waymo claims that they've done well-over 5 billion miles of simulated roadway testing via computer-based simulations, encompassing 10,000 virtual self-driving cars. The nice thing about a simulation is that you can just keep running it and running it. No need to stop. Now, there is of course a cost involved in using whatever computers or supercomputer is doing the simulation, and so that can be a barrier to be contended with in terms of how much simulations you are able to do. Generally, one might say the more the merrier, in terms of simulations, assuming that you are not just simulating the same thing over and over again.

Another variant on the use of simulations involves situations wherein the AI self-driving car has gotten into an incident and you want to do a post-mortem (or, you should have done what I call a pre-mortem). You can setup the simulator to try and recreate the situation that occurred with the AI self-driving car. It might then reveal aspects about how the accident occurred and ways to possibly prevent such accidents in the future. The results of the simulation could be used to then have the AI developers modify the AI systems and push a patch out to the AI on-board the self-driving cars.

Should an auto maker or tech firm go out and buy an exascale supercomputer? It's hard to say whether the cost would be worthwhile to them in terms of their AI self-driving car efforts. They might already have a supercomputer that they use for the overall design of their cars, along with simulations associated with their cars (this is done with conventional cars too). Or, they might rent use of a supercomputer.

I had mentioned earlier that I would point out that you don't necessarily need to buy a supercomputer to use one. For the research oriented supercomputers being developed at universities, they often allow requests to make use of the supercomputer, if there's a bona fide reason to do so. The University of Manchester's neuromorphic supercomputer can be used for doing research by others beyond just those directly involved in the existing efforts (you just need to file a request and if approved you can make use of it). IBM provides the "IBM Q Experience" wherein you can potentially get access to their quantum computer to tryout various programs on it.

If someone is really serious about using a supercomputer on a sustaining basis, the costs can begin to mount. You'd need to do an ROI (Return on Investment) analysis to figure out whether it is better to rent time or potentially buy one. As mentioned before, the outright cost of buying a supercomputer is pretty much only within reach for very large companies and governmental agencies. The good news is that with the emergence of the Internet and cloud computing, you can readily make use of tremendous computing power that was once very hard to reach and utilize.

For AI self-driving cars, there is value in having supercomputing that can be used for doing behind-the-scenes work such as performing simulations and doing data analyses, along with aiding in doing Machine Learning. A more advanced approach involves having the AI self-driving cars being able to tap into the supercomputing and use it in real-time or near real-time circumstances. This real-time aspect is quite tricky and requires a lot of checks-and-balances, including making sure that doing so does not inadvertently open up a security hole.

The amount of computing power put into an AI self-driving car is almost the same as having your very own "supercomputer" in your self-driving car (that's if you are willing to consider that you will have nearly as much computer processing as the early days of supercomputers). You aren't though going to have a modern-day exascale supercomputer inside your AI self-driving car (at least not yet!). As the joke goes, your AI self-driving car is able to compute so quickly that it can do an infinite loop in less than 5 seconds, and with the help of a true exascale supercomputer get it done in less than 1 second. Glad that I was able to resurrect that one.

CHAPTER 3

SUPERHUMAN AI AND AI SELF-DRIVING CARS

CHAPTER 3

SUPERHUMAN AI AND
AI SELF-DRIVING CARS

I have a beef about the now seemingly in-vogue use of the "superhuman AI" phrase that keeps popping up in the media. When I was asked about "superhuman AI" at a recent Machine Learning and AI industry conference, I admit that I wound myself up into a bit of a tizzy and launched into a modest diatribe. Now that I've calmed down, I thought you might like to know what my angst is about the so-called superhuman AI moniker and why it is important to give the matter of its use some serious consideration.

Have you noticed the phrase? It can be subtle and at times easy to miss. I'd guess that if you look around, you'll see that the superhuman AI phrase might have been in any of a number of recent articles you have read about AI breakthroughs, or might have gotten mentioned during a radio broadcast or on a podcast that you listen to while in your car. If so, I realize you might have not given it any thought at all.

In that sense, you could argue that the superhuman AI phrase is not consequential and there's no reason to get upset about its use. It is perhaps a kind of filler phrase that sounds good and hopefully most people know it likely lacks any substantive true meaning. Just more noise and nothing noteworthy.

On the other hand, there is a potential danger that this superhuman AI phrase is indeed being taken quite seriously by those that are not well familiar with AI, and thus it can tend to overinflate what AI can actually achieve. There are some in AI that seem to be pleased to inflate expectations about AI, but fortunately there are moderates that rightfully worry that these subtle attempts at overstating AI are going to get everyone into trouble.

The trouble can be that we all begin to believe that AI can do things it cannot and then allow ourselves to become vulnerable to automated systems that really have no bearing on this mythical and made-up notion of today's AI.

I'll make a bold statement herein and claim that by-and-large when someone reports that they have developed an AI system that is characterized by superhuman AI, they are generally being misleading. It could be marketing hype. It could be personal bravado. It could be they are purposely or possibly even inadvertently are deploying hyperbole. It could be that the person is naïve. It could be that they are unknowingly overstating things. It could be that they don't care whether their statements are accurate or not. Etc.

They might also believe that for *their* definition of superhuman AI, they are reasonably making use of the phrase.

This does bring up a bit of a conundrum about the superhuman AI phrase.

There is not an across the board all-agreed standardized and codified definition that everyone has said that yes, this is what superhuman AI consists of. Nobody has laid out precise and demonstrable metrics that we should use to decide concretely whether there is or is not superhuman AI involved. Therefore, with no specific rules to be followed, you can use the phrase however you might wish. There isn't a kind of word-usage cop standing by the roadside that has an improper-AI-phrases radar gun that can detect the true and proper use of the superhuman AI phrase. It is instead a wild west.

You can even fiendishly use the phrase to suggest or imply with a wink-wink that there is really a lot of super-duper AI in your system, but at the same time claim when pressed that you were intending to use it in a less-than over-the-top manner. The looseness of the existing commonplace unstated definition allows for making what you want of the handy and catchy phrase and gives you face-saving wiggle room to do so.

Let's consider what the phrase potentially means.

The first word, superhuman, we all generally would agree means to accomplish something of an extraordinary nature beyond what a normal human might be able to do. The other day a man lifted a car because his child had gotten pinned underneath it. Normally, it is doubtful that he could lift a car by himself. He somehow gained momentarily a kind of superhuman strength, perhaps due to adrenalin running through his body, and was able to lift that car.

You could say that he was superhuman. But, does this mean that in all respects he is superhuman? Can he lift a building like superman? No. Could he even lift a car again? Unlikely, unless his child once again got stuck underneath one. For all reasonable notions of superhuman, I think we could say that he momentarily displayed an extraordinary strength that a normal person might not typically have.

He wasn't therefore a now-permanent superhuman that forever would have this super strength. He did not arrive here from the plant Krypton. Instead, he momentarily appeared to engage in an activity that most of us would probably be willing to say seems relatively superhuman-like.

Suppose though that we went out and found a really strong weight lifter and asked that person to lift the same car as the man that had been saving his child. If the strong lifter could do so, is that strong lifter also then someone that we would immediately applaud as being superhuman? I'd suggest we would not.

This brings up the aspect that when we refer to someone as superhuman, we probably need to have some basis for comparison.

If the basis for comparison is solely confined to what the particular person could normally do, this would seem to quite dilute the idea of being superhuman. I tried to open a screw-top can the other day and could not do so. I tried and tried. A few days later, I tried again and managed to squirm and grunt and got that darned lid to turn and come off. I was now superhuman!

I don't think that it seems fair or reasonable to say that I was superhuman in that case. Big deal, I opened a screw-top can that was somewhat jammed up. A lot of humans could do the same. Just because I was able to exceed my prior effort, it doesn't seem to warrant handing me a trophy as being superhuman. I think you would likely agree.

It was Friedrich Nietzsche that many suggest first helped to bolster the notion of someone potentially being superhuman. You might become superhuman by perhaps being genetically bred in a manner that gives you greater strength or greater intelligence than other humans. Or, maybe you have a cybernetic implant inserted into your body that gives you superhuman strength, or you take special drugs that make your mind more powerful and superhuman, similar to what is often portrayed in many science fiction movies.

There is a slippery slope between talking about superhuman and contemplating the aspects of Superman or Superwoman. The word "super" is used in the case of superhuman, and can allude to having super powers, and so you then start to think of Superman or Superwoman, which even though they don't exist and are only fictional characters, nonetheless the superhuman word gets the glow from those now ubiquitous fake characters. It is easy to therefore mentally get intertwined that "superhuman = superman or superwoman," which is part of the reason that superhuman is a lousy word and distorts our sense of what is real and what is not.

In spite of the troubles associated with the meaning of the word superhuman, we'll go ahead and add to the mess by appending the "AI" moniker to the superhuman word.

Superhuman AI. Now what do we mean?

If I develop a tic-tac-toe game that uses AI techniques and even executes on so-called AI hardware, can I claim that my tic-tac-toe game is superhuman AI?

I wouldn't think so. But, I assure you, there are some that would happily say it is. It's the best darned tic-tac-toe game player ever devised. It exceeds anyone else in being able to play tic-tac-toe. It will never ever lose a tic-tac-toe game. Must be AI. Probably a breakthrough. Must be superhuman AI.

Where this especially seems to come up about using the phrase superhuman AI is when referring to automated systems that play games. Automated systems have been developed for chess that have been able to beat human grand masters and reach new heights of human chess play scoring. Some say that's superhuman AI.

Top playing automated systems for Scrabble reached a zenith around 2006. Superhuman AI. More recently, in 2016, an automated system was a winner at Go, considered by many to have been a nearly unreachable goal due to the nature of the rules of Go and the kinds of strategies used. Superhuman AI. You've all likely seen the plentiful ads for the IBM Watson about the winning at Jeopardy. Superhuman AI.

I want to outright congratulate those that were able to get automated systems to play at such a vaunted human level in those games. They used every computer science and AI technique and novelty to get to that accomplishment. Here, here!

Were those all superhuman AI examples?

Some say that games are great as a means to perfect many AI and computer science techniques and approaches, but they are quite narrow in their domains.

There are games with perfect information, meaning that you are informed of all events that occur throughout the playing of the game, knowing each of the moves as they arise and the starting position.

Chess is an example of having "perfect" information since you know how the game starts and you know each move that occurs along the way. Players don't somehow hide their moves. Also, there isn't any "chance" involved in the game since there isn't dice or something else being used to determine what the moves are. It is straight ahead. Imperfect information games are those not within the definition of a perfect information game.

Does playing games well or even extraordinarily with an automated system mean that it is superhuman AI?

Suppose that we don't use any special AI techniques at all, and merely leverage having a much vaster amount of online storage available than a human could likely have in their mind, and we do a great job at searching an extremely large space of pre-calculated best moves (having been precalculated by human led direction for the automated system).

Is it fair to toss the "AI" into the superhuman wording?

Let's consider domains beyond those of playing games.

I had helped an assembly plant put a robotic arm into their assembly line, doing so to speed-up the line and reduce the labor needed to produce their product. Most would agree that the field of robotics generally fits within the overarching definition of AI.

I'd like to brag about the robotic arm work, but admittedly the mechanical arm was merely trained by having a human move the arm back-and-forth until it caught onto the movements needed. I also added various safety related code to make sure the robotic arm wouldn't go astray. It was a nice project and would also reduce the various repetitive motion injuries that the human workers had been experiencing while doing the same task. I also trained the former assembly worker how to take care of the robotic arm and be able to make changes and updates to the code as needed.

Was the robotic arm that I helped customize and got working an example of a superhuman AI accomplishment?

Yes, you could apparently make such a claim.

It used robotics, which as mentioned generally fits within the AI rubric. It was superhuman because it can easily beat any human at the assembly line task. Whereas before a human could do the overall task about six times per hour, the robotic arm could nearly double that pace (about 10 times per hour). The robotic arm could work 24x7, no need to rest or relax or take breaks. For all practical purposes, you could assert that it was superhuman in comparison to what a human could do. You could say it was superhuman beyond any other human, since no human could possibly unaided by machinery work like that.

Personally, it would give me heartburn to go around and say that this robotic arm was superhuman AI. But, that's just me.

You might say that physical things don't count for the superhuman AI moniker. In the case of the robotic arm, it wasn't "thinking" in any superhuman kind of way. Therefore, maybe we should only use superhuman AI when the matter at-hand involves thinking, akin to winning at chess or Scrabble.

Does the superhuman AI have to be the best in comparison to all humans? In other words, if we construct an AI system that plays chess, and it beats the topmost human chess players, we might then assert or infer that it can beat all humans in that domain and therefore it is rightfully superhuman.

If it cannot beat all humans in the domain, what then?

Someone develops a Machine Learning capability that is able to diagnose MRI's and find cancerous regions, doing so more consistently than the average medical doctor and at times better than the best medical specialists in that domain. Let's assume we cannot say it is always better than all humans in that respect. It is only sometimes better.

Superhuman AI?

Some suggest that we ought to have a graduated series of categories that lead-up to being referred to as superhuman.

We might do this:

- Superhuman AI = better than all humans in the domain, as far as we can so infer

- High-human AI = better than most humans in the domain, high as in heightened

- Par-human AI = similar to most humans in the domain or "on par" with humans

- Subpar-human AI = less than or worse than most humans in the domain, sub-par

Notice that I've qualified the superhuman in two important respects, one by the aspect of saying it pertains to a particular domain, and the other that we can only infer that the AI in that case is better than all humans in the domain.

The latter assumption is due to the aspect that we cannot really say whether or not the AI might be better than all humans (unless we really can have all human's line-up and showcase that none are better than the AI, all 7.5 billion people on the planet).

Let's take chess. Just because you can beat the most recent top-rated chess masters does not mean you can beat all humans in chess. There might be someone that is a chess wizard that nobody even knows exists. Or, maybe next week a chess wizard appears seemingly out of nowhere that can play chess better than any other human on Earth. Thus, we'll have to approximate that based on whatever kind of circumstance is involved, such as with chess, we'll say that the AI is better than "all" humans but do so knowing that we are making a bit of a leap-in-faith on that aspect.

Some react to the superhuman AI by believing that the superhuman AI can do anything in any field of endeavor. That's why I've put into the aforementioned indications that it is the AI within the domain of choice, such as chess or Go.

This is also why the superhuman AI moniker is on that slippery slope. If you tell someone that you have superhuman AI that can play chess, they might think this implies that AI can play any kind of game to that same topmost level, since we all know that chess is hard and therefore presumably the AI can just switch over and be superhuman at say Monopoly (which most people would say is a lot less arduous than chess and so it should be "easy" presumably for a superhuman AI chess playing system to win at Monopoly).

Of course, today's so-called superhuman AI instances are all within a narrow domain and do not have an ability to just switch over on their own and be tops at other domains.

Worse still, some people that hear about something that is superhuman AI will often ascribe to the matter that is must also have common sense reasoning and also Artificial General Intelligence (AGI). If it can play chess so well, it likely can solve world hunger or clean-up our environment too. Nope, sorry about that but those aren't in the cards right now.

What does this have to do with AI self-driving cars?

At the Cybernetic AI Self-Driving Car Institute, we are developing AI software for self-driving cars. There are some within the self-driving driverless car industry that are either using the phrase "superhuman AI" or are letting others use that phrase for them.

Is the superhuman AI moniker applicable to aspects of today's AI self-driving cars?

Allow me to elaborate.

I'd like to first clarify and introduce the notion that there are varying levels of AI self-driving cars. The topmost level is considered Level 5. A Level 5 self-driving car is one that is being driven by the AI and there is no human driver involved. For the design of Level 5 self-driving cars, the auto makers are even removing the gas pedal, brake pedal, and steering wheel, since those are contraptions used by human drivers. The Level 5 self-driving car is not being driven by a human and nor is there an expectation that a human driver will be present in the self-driving car. It's all on the shoulders of the AI to drive the car.

For self-driving cars less than a Level 5, there must be a human driver present in the car. The human driver is currently considered the responsible party for the acts of the car. The AI and the human driver are co-sharing the driving task. In spite of this co-sharing, the human is supposed to remain fully immersed into the driving task and be ready at all times to perform the driving task. I've repeatedly warned about the dangers of this co-sharing arrangement and predicted it will produce many untoward results.

Let's focus herein on the true Level 5 self-driving car. Much of the comments apply to the less than Level 5 self-driving cars too, but the fully autonomous AI self-driving car will receive the most attention in this discussion.

Here's the usual steps involved in the AI driving task:

- Sensor data collection and interpretation
- Sensor fusion
- Virtual world model updating
- AI action planning
- Car controls command issuance

Another key aspect of AI self-driving cars is that they will be driving on our roadways in the midst of human driven cars too. There are some pundits of AI self-driving cars that continually refer to a utopian world in which there are only AI self-driving cars on the public roads. Currently there are about 250+ million conventional cars in the United

States alone, and those cars are not going to magically disappear or become true Level 5 AI self-driving cars overnight.

Indeed, the use of human driven cars will last for many years, likely many decades, and the advent of AI self-driving cars will occur while there are still human driven cars on the roads. This is a crucial point since this means that the AI of self-driving cars needs to be able to contend with not just other AI self-driving cars, but also contend with human driven cars. It is easy to envision a simplistic and rather unrealistic world in which all AI self-driving cars are politely interacting with each other and being civil about roadway interactions. That's not what is going to be happening for the foreseeable future. AI self-driving cars and human driven cars will need to be able to cope with each other.

Returning to the superhuman AI discussion, let's consider how this catchy phrase is being used by some in today's AI self-driving car industry.

For the sensors side of things, it seems like anytime an improvement is made in being able to analyze an image and detect whether there is say a pedestrian in a picture, there is someone that will claim the AI or ML based capability is superhuman AI. This seems to suggest that if the shape of a pedestrian can be picked-out of a hazy image, it is somehow better than a human's ability to do human-based image analysis. Rarely is there much substantive support provided for such a contention.

Furthermore, given the relatively brittle nature of most of today's image processing capabilities, even if the new routine can do a better job at that one particular aspect, one has to ask whether this is a fair and reasonable way to then ascribe to it that it is superhuman AI. We all know that a human could do a much broader scope kind of image analysis and likely "best" the image processing software in an overall effort of doing image detection.

We also know that the image processing software has no "understanding" whatsoever about the image that it has detected. It has found a shape and associated it with something within the system tagged as a pedestrian. Does it "know" that a pedestrian is a human being that breaths and walks and lives and thinks? No. Does it "know" that a pedestrian might suddenly run or jump or shout at the self-driving car? No.

Yet, it is superhuman AI?

For those AI developers that would argue that it is superhuman AI, I'll simply repeat my earlier qualm that for those that aren't aware of AI's limitations and constraints as it exists today, your willingness to toss around the superhuman AI moniker is going to get someone in trouble. The public will falsely believe that the AI of the self-driving car is more sophisticated and more capable than it really is. Regulators are going to falsely believe that the AI of the self-driving car is more robust and safer than it really is. And so on, down the line for all of the stakeholders involved in AI self-driving cars.

I'd be willing to bet that this wanton use of "superhuman AI" will ultimately come to the spotlight when there are product liability lawsuits lobbed against the auto makers and tech firms that brandished such wording. Didn't the "superhuman AI" mislead consumers into believing that their AI self-driving car could do things that it really could not, will be a question asked during the case. By what manner did you arrive at being able to proclaim that your AI self-driving car had this kind of superhuman AI, will be another question. And so on.

Some argue that being perhaps over-the-top is the only way to make sure that funding and energy continues to pore into the AI field.

Presumably, a bit of hyperbole is worth the "cost" as it provides an overwhelming goodness when considered as a trade-off to otherwise losing steam and momentum in the quest to reach true AI. If we went around and told people that we are in the midst of AI systems that are par-human, or subpar-human, it might be a shock that would undermine investments and faith in pushing ahead with AI.

Superhuman AI seems like a modest enough phrase that it can be used without having an abundance of guilt or misgivings, at least for some. You'll have to make that decision on your own and live with it.

Fortunately, I don't think you need to be superhuman to make the right decision about this.

CHAPTER 4

OLFACTORY E-NOSE SENSORS AND AI SELF-DRIVING CARS

Lance B. Eliot

CHAPTER 4

OLFACTORY E-NOSE SENSORS AND AI SELF-DRIVING CARS

Consider for a moment your nose. Yes, your nose. The human nose has an amazing capability to detect odors and remains as one of the "last frontier" areas for trying to duplicate this same functionality into an electronic sensor of some kind. If you have an idea of how to make a fully capable e-nose, an electronic nose, you could be sitting on a goldmine.

Light sensors such as cameras are pretty well matured and can readily take the energy wavelengths of light and capture it for us. Sound sensors such as microphones are pretty well matured and can readily take the energy of sound and capture it for us. Odors are trickier because the nose functions by detecting molecules representing odors, which becomes a form of mass measurement rather than energy measurement. Attempts to develop e-nose devices have generally met with difficulty and perfecting a bioelectronic nose or machine olfaction is still an open avenue awaiting a breakthrough.

The interaction of the physiological aspects of the nose and the psychological aspects of the brain are a wonderment.

As an example, the other day I was walking through a farmer's market in downtown Los Angeles and was joyfully taking a look at the dozens upon dozens of food items that were on display and being cooked, trying to decide what I might eat for lunch that day. Wafting through the air of the marketplace was a cacophony of odors. I could smell slowly roasting meats, I could detect the distinct odor of veggies being cooked, and so on.

All of a sudden, I got a whiff of an odor that caught me by surprise. It was a scent that I had not smelled in many years. My parents used to make a certain kind of unusual soup for special occasions when we had guests come to our home, and I had not ever seen or smelled the scent of that soup since I was a very young child. With just the tiniest hint of the smell in the farmer's market, my mind raced back to the days of my childhood and I remembered vividly the times when the cooking of the soup took all day long and occurred in anticipation of out-of-town visitors coming to our home for dinner.

It was incredible that with the miniscule whiff of this odor that I suddenly was transported back in time to my childhood and inescapably a somewhat obscure memory took over my mind momentarily.

That's the grand power of our noses. They can smell pleasant odors such as perfumes, colognes, and other pleasing fragrances. As humans, we obviously seem to give importance to such odors because the estimated global market is about $75 billion being spent annually for fragrances (according to Statista). That's a lot of money for merely giving our noses something sweet to smell. There must be something significant about our noses to justify that kind of spending.

The other side of the smelling activity involves those rotten and horrid odors that repulse us.

The other night in my neighborhood there was a skunk smell that seemed to last for nearly an hour. When the odor first became apparent, I was outdoors and decided I'd try to avoid the smell by going inside my house. The windows of my house were open and shortly the entire house had the stink of the skunk in it.

I even thought that the skunk must be right under my floorboards or be purposely standing at my window and emanating the stench from there. I was torn as to whether to now close the windows, perhaps trapping the odor inside, or even open them wider in hopes that the prevailing winds might blow through the house and get the odor out. What a pickle!

The skunk uses odors as a defensive mechanism. This highlights again the power of smells. We all might think it obvious that an animal might use claws or teeth as a defensive tool, but the idea of simply using an odor seems less useful to our overall sensibility about ways to protect yourself. Emit an odor and somehow prevent other creatures from trying to devour you? Doesn't at first seem like a credible idea.

Keep in mind that if you get too close to a skunk odor, you can get nauseous and your eyes can burn from the odor. Thus, their odorous defense is more than simply causing you to be discomforted by the unpleasant smell -- most animals seem to realize that messing around with a skunk is going to be a bad move for them. Besides skunks, various other animals also use odors to their advantage, including bombardier beetles that use odors for defensive purposes and opossums are also able to use odors for repelling predators (it's via their excrement).

I had mentioned that while in the farmer's market I had gotten just a faint whiff of the soup odor that launched me into going down memory lane. Our noses can often pick-up very faint odors that are at a distance or that are very diluted in the air. The skunk odor near my house was at first rather slim, but eventually it became nearly overpowering and I was almost choking on the stink.

We can categorize odors by their intensity, such as this scale is often used:

0 = no odor detected

1 = very weak odor and at threshold of detection

2 = weak odor that is considered detected

3 = distinct odor that is considered fully detected

4 = strong odor

5 = very strong odor

6 = intolerable odor overpowering (some say "suffocating")

It's not just the intensity that governs the nature of our nose and its ability to smell odors, but also the type of odor that counts too.

There is some dispute about whether or not there are "primary" odors, akin to the notion of having primary colors. Smells are not quite as readily categorized as what we can see via light. Some also assert that smells are much more subjective and that the "eye of the beholder" comes to play in the manner of the "nose of the besmeller" (Ok, that's a Shakespearean word), determines whether an odor is pleasant or not.

When my children were young, I used to change their diapers as babies and the smell was quite rough to withstand. A friend of mine that also had children, he loved the smell of his kids filled-up diapers.

He used to brag about the odors and even wished that he could capture the smells and preserve them, similar to taking pictures and putting those into a photo album. I loved my kids, but the packed fully "perfumed" diaper was not the top of my list of awesome odors.

Anyway, some researchers list these below seven aspects as a proposed list of primary smells, take a look and see if you agree that these are the core odors of the world:

1. Musky
2. Putrid (such as the odor or rotten eggs)
3. Pungent (vinegar would be an example)
4. Camphoraceous (mothball-like odors)
5. Ethereal (an example would-be dry-cleaning fluid)
6. Floral (a rose by any other name)
7. Pepperminty

A catchy mnemonic for considering the nature of odors is FIDOL.

The F stands for the frequency of the odor. The I is the intensity of the odor (which I've provided an intensity rating system herein). The letter D is for the duration or length of time that the odor exists for you to smell it. The use of the letter O refers to the offensiveness of the odor. And the letter L is used to indicate that the Location of the odor can be significant.

In studies of fruit flies, we are able to learn quite a bit about how odors seem to work and reveal aspects about how the "nose" functions.

An interesting study done at the University of California San Diego and in conjunction with the Salk Institute for Biological Studies revealed that a fruit fly seems to tag each odor that it detects. Tags are then placed into one of two overall buckets, an attractiveness group or a repulsive group. The tags are somewhat sparse and non-overlapping.

The appearance of an odor gets the nostril receptors to become chemically stimulated. This stimulus then generates electrical kinds of biological signals that are then transmitted to the brain. There are Odor Receptor Neurons (ORN) used for this purpose.

The fruit fly study was especially intriguing because it seems that the fruit fly first does the odor detection with about 50 neurons, and then it fans them out to a wider set of about 2,000 neurons. This would seem counter-intuitive because you would usually expect that an odor would fan down, being narrowed so as to figure out the nature of the particular odor.

The researchers likened this fanning expansion as the equivalent to having a bunch of people in a crowded room, whereby you could not readily make heads nor tails of each person because they are crammed together, and instead you repositioned them onto a football field. By repositioning them into a large open space, you would have an easier time of being able to categorize them and figure out what you seem to have in-hand. That's the working theory on it.

What also made this intriguing was that the researchers suggest that the fruit fly olfactory circuitry uses a kind of locality-sensitive hashing (LSH) function, which is a known form of a computer science algorithm for search-space purposes. Presumably, the fruit fly assigns tags to an odor and for which the more similar the two tags are the greater chances of realizing that those are odors of a similar nature (thus, being "locality-sensitive"). This is akin to being able to numerically find the approximate and nearest neighbors in a highly dimensional search space using a hashing function. Nice to see that perhaps the programming we do with computers can be seen as something that nature itself has honed and uses too (yes, I realize that nature's version came first!).

What about humans and their ability to differentiate various odors?

Another study done on olfactory senses involved using Machine Learning (ML) to try and identify and predict which molecules would lead to which kinds of human-determined smells. Done by researchers at several universities including The Rockefeller University and Arizona State University, they were trying to see whether it might be possible to predict a "smell" by the molecules that presumably should invoke the human-determined and described odor.

This is crucial since right now there is little in the way of well characterizing the dimensionality and size of the olfactory perception space, and furthermore the range and nature of the invoking odors is itself a hazy kind stimulus space.

I liked this particular study since it suggests that we can construct models to be able to take a "subjective" smell and reverse engineer it back to the likely molecules that caused the odor. Plus, we can potentially inspect a molecule and be able to somewhat accurately predict what kind of smell that people will think it has. The Machine Learning approach was augmented by a regularized linear model that did nearly as good at the predictions as did a more elaborated random forest version.

These kinds of studies are all small steps toward trying to unravel the mysteries of our noses and the act of smelling.

Of course, research has been going on for many decades to try and ferret out how we smell something. I don't want you to think that research is only just now occurring. It is an age-old quest to unlock the secrets of the nose. What makes these more recent studies a rather hopeful effort, and especially worthy of renewed attention is that we have the techniques and technologies today that can allow us to perform research and potentially make a true e-nose, which in years past would have been nearly impossible to do or much harder because the software and hardware were not yet ready for such an effort.

Odors and our noses are part of our primal senses.

Nature has cooked into us this phenomenal thing that we call a nose. Your nose can detect odors that might warn you of impending dangers. Your nose can help you to locate a suitable mate (that's why there is so much perfume being bought!). In a caveman and cavewoman kind of way, we have used our noses to find food, along with using our noses to detect potential predators.

Anyone that has gone hunting knows that you should try to stay downwind of a bear or deer, since otherwise they might detect your human odor and scoot away. The same can be said for humans, namely that we try to smell whether a predator is nearby, though our ability to detect odors is not as superpowered as many animals (think about this as you walk your dog around the neighborhood and it is constantly sniffing at the air and at objects).

Humans seem to vary in terms of the ability to smell odors. I'm betting you know people that when you ask them whether they can smell a particular odor, they say they cannot, and yet for you it is overpowering. One such example was an office that I used to work in. Every late afternoon, a fellow worker would put popcorn into the microwave and cook it until it burnt. The burnt odor was excessive and permeated the entire office. When I asked my fellow office workers if the odor disturbed them, most said they could barely smell it. When I asked the person that made the popcorn whether they felt any guilt in imposing the burnt odor onto the rest of us, he said that he enjoyed the odor and thought it perked up the atmosphere of the office.

It seems that we all have our own subjective indicators about odors. Some claim that women can smell odors that men cannot or at least are more sensitive to certain odors. Thus, there might be a gender difference in the ability to smell. Some say that the older you get, the less sensitive you are to odors. This might suggest an age-related factor to odor detection. Health is another factor as to whether your nose can aptly identify smells.

There is odor fatigue that comes to play too. If you are exposed to an odor continuously, there is a chance that your nose will gradually begin to stop reacting to the odor and so the odor will appear to fade, even though it might still be heavily present. For the burnt popcorn, I reluctantly tolerated the daily afternoon smell-fest, and kind of got used to it over time. When we had guests come and visit the office, doing so in the late afternoon, invariably they would react quite strongly upon first detecting the smell. Our first exposure to a smell can be strongest and then fade after we get used to an odor.

Another example of getting used to an odor and no longer noticing it includes our own personal body odors. I went camping for a week as part of the Boy Scouts, doing so as a troop leader. We were in the woods and didn't readily have available a shower or other ways to bathe. After a few days, the odors of each of the troop members was readily detected. You could be standing behind a tree and indicate who was on the other side of the tree, simply by their body odor. The person themselves often didn't even think they had a detectable body odor and it was hard to convince them that they stunk like a skunk.

When you ask someone to try and pinpoint an odor, it can be challenging at times. Assuming that they indeed smell the odor, there is a kind of search in their minds about the nature of the odor. Most people can usually tell you rather quickly whether they have ever smelled the odor before. We seem to have a cognitive ability to rapidly do a search of our mental space to see whether an odor has ever been recorded in our minds.

If you then ask the person what the odor means or signifies, they often need to do more mental searching. It might be difficult for the person to remember when or where they last had smelled the odor. It is as though cognitively the "records" associated with the odor are poorly linked together. Perhaps over time the neural connections to the stored odor have faded or changed or been used for some other purposes. Trying to make a reconnection can require some deep concentration, perhaps a means of the mind trying to do a search and then reinvigorate prior connections or create new ones based on the reconstruction of past events.

What's even less likely consists of having someone tell you what the odor consists of. For a skunk, it is pretty much just the odor of a skunk. If you've got a Starbucks fancy coffee, you might be able to pick out the odors of the coffee and the various added ingredients, assuming you've trained yourself to do so or otherwise paid attention to the concoction and memorized what the various components smelled like.

You've perhaps seen wine tasters that claim they can tell you not only the elements of the wine based on smelling it, they often impress by telling you the year of the wine, where it was made, and try to do a James Bond kind of thing by saying they can even tell you the name of the person that stomped on the grapes.

People though that swear they can smell numerous distinct components of an overall odor can at times be falsely thinking that they do. I'm not necessarily saying that the person is lying. It could be that the person genuinely believes they detect various odors, but it is a kind of trick of the mind that they believe this.

You can tell a person that they are holding a coffee with certain ingredients, and they affirm the ingredients by sniffing the coffee, but meanwhile you've handed them the wrong cup of coffee and it doesn't have those items in it at all. Their mind had led them to believe that the elements were there, and so it might have imputed the odors even when they were not there at all.

One odor can at times overpower another odor, causing you to lose your ability to detect the now hidden odor. If I put one of those filled-up diapers next to a Starbucks coffee, I assure you that you would not likely be waxing on and on about how great the coffee smelled. In any complex mixture of odors, the ability to pick out specific odors can be quite hard to do. You've likely seen people sniff something, tell you an odor, then sniff the item again, and tell you another odor. At times, we can perhaps mentally isolate one odor from a mixture, if we put our minds to it.

Speaking of the mind, once the Odor Receptor Neurons report an odor to the brain, it's up to the mind to figure out what the odor is and what significance it might have. Since this is a mental matter, you can presumably alter your thinking about an odor and become more attracted to it or more repulsed by it, over time. I had a dog that at first was smelly and I didn't want to use perfume-like soap to mask the odor. Gradually, I got used to the natural odor and even liked the smell. Even today, if I smell a dog that has a similar such odor, I get a big smile as it reminds me of that favored dog that I once had.

Odors can have a tremendous impact on our emotions and ultimately our behavior. I say this because sometimes when I talk about an olfactory e-nose sensor, there are people that shrug off the sense of smell as a kind of irrelevant topic. If you ask these people about their various senses, they would say that their eyes and ears are crucial, but their nose is not. Were their nose to get plugged up and be unusable, they would say it doesn't particular matter to them. No big deal.

Aromatherapy claims that you can cure various psychological and physiological ills of the body by paying attention to odors and the proper use of odors. It is at times startling to be reminded out-of-the-blue about the power of the nose and the nature of odors. My farmer's market experience was an example of how the body and mind work together at times. The moment that I sniffed the odor in that farmer's market and separated it from the many other odors wafting through the thick air, my mind leapt back to my childhood, resurrecting memories that I doubt I could have otherwise readily recalled, even if you asked me to do so. An odor and the functions of the nose and the mind can be rather incredible.

I would say that sometimes odors can be lifesaving.

During one of the Scouting trips, I was driving my car through a vast wooded wilderness, trying to connect up with my troop. I had been delayed at work getting to the campsite and so was arriving long after everyone else had arrived and setup camp. The roads were all dirt roads and there was no particular signage and certainly no GPS available in this remote area. It was getting toward sunset and the darkness would make it even harder to find where the troop was camped out.

I had the windows rolled down, in case I might be able to hear the sounds of the troop. Often, you can hear the troop leaders barking out orders or hear the sound of the Scouts exploring the woods. My eyes were peeled, looking for any kind of indication that maybe the troop was around the next bend. I began to smell an odor, the smell of smoke, a campfire.

I realized that the troop would have setup a campfire and it would likely be the only one anywhere near to this area of the empty wilderness. I used my nose to try and catch the odor. I even put my head outside of the driver's side window, and sure enough was able to figure out which road to take to get to the campsite. The nose came to the rescue!

I realize you might say that this example was not a lifesaver per se, since I would have been unlikely to somehow expire if I did not find the campsite. Yes, I could have survived in my car for the night and then gone to look for them the next day (actually, I would likely have setup my own miniature camp, using my brought along camping gear!).

Here's some examples that might be more relevant to the notion of being lifesaving.

I was with a bunch of the troop members while driving toward a campout that we were going to have for just a weekend. The weather conditions were quite dry. It was summer time and the temperature was in the high 90's or low 100's during the day. Other parts of the local mountains had unfortunately had fires recently, so we were concerned generally about a potential forest fire. Nonetheless, we had scheduled to go camping for that weekend and figured we'd give it a try.

We had driven up after work on a Friday, and so it was nighttime when we arrived at the wilderness. There was no lighting on any of the dirt roads. The only light available was via the headlights of the car. There were several other cars behind me, all part of our caravan headed up to camping for the weekend.

Coming along a winding mountainous road, we began to just barely detect a smoke-like odor. It was very faint. In fact, at first, I didn't say anything about it. I thought that my awareness of the other forest fires was playing tricks on my mind. Some of the troop members in my car spoke-up and asked if anyone else could smell smoke. I was relieved that they said something, and it wasn't just in my own mind.

I was going very slowly on this winding road since it was replete with ruts and holes, and we were on a cliff that if you made a wrong move would mean a car would go over the side and down to its doom. As we inched ahead, everyone agreed that the smoky odor was getting stronger and stronger. We didn't see anything up ahead and were perplexed that we could not see flames shooting up into the air. Nor could we see the smoke, though it was nighttime and so dark that we could barely see our hands in front of our faces.

I decided that where there is smoke, there is fire (well, that's true a lot of the time), so I opted to turnaround the car. I slowly drove back down and reached the other cars that were still making their way up. Since I was the lead car, there weren't any other cars ahead of me. Upon meeting up with those other cars, we told them about the smoke odor and how it was progressively getting stronger. We all agreed that it made sense to head back down out of the mountains as a precaution.

The next day, we found out that a fire had gotten started up in that region and it eventually became a widespread forest fire. Had we kept going and opted to campout, we might have gotten stuck in it and the thought of endangering our lives still somewhat haunts me that we might have done so, had we not luckily smelled the smoke when the fire was just starting to burn.

Okay, so that's hopefully more of a lifesaving example.

Here's another one, a bit quicker of a story. I was driving and pulled into a gas station. I was going to stop and pump some gas, but I immediately upon getting near the pump, I could smell a heavy odor of gasoline. I decided to drive straight out of the gas station and not stop. As I drove onto the street, I looked back and could see that someone had spilled a bunch of gasoline onto the ground near to the pumps. All it would have taken was one spark and the situation could have been awful.

I don't want you to think that detecting odors while in your car is only about lifesaving. The other morning, I was driving on a highway and came to a red light. As I sat there, I could distinctly smell the pleasant scent of baked goods. Sure enough, there was a bakery at the corner, one that I had never particularly noticed because it was a small and inconspicuous mom-and-pop bakery. I made a U-turn and came back over to check it out. Turns out it is now one of my favored locations to get freshly baked blueberry muffins and other pastries.

What does this have to do with AI self-driving cars?

At the Cybernetic AI Self-Driving Car Institute, we are developing AI software for self-driving cars.

A key element for AI self-driving cars are the various sensors that detect the world surrounding the self-driving car. These include sensors for capturing video and still images, along with radar sensors, LIDAR sensors, ultrasonic sensors, and the like. One futuristic sensor that is intriguing notion would be an olfactory sensor, an e-nose for your AI self-driving car.

I'd like to clarify and introduce the notion that there are varying levels of AI self-driving cars. The topmost level is considered Level 5. A Level 5 self-driving car is one that is being driven by the AI and there is no human driver involved. For the design of Level 5 self-driving cars, the auto makers are even removing the gas pedal, brake pedal, and steering wheel, since those are contraptions used by human drivers. The Level 5 self-driving car is not being driven by a human and nor is there an expectation that a human driver will be present in the self-driving car. It's all on the shoulders of the AI to drive the car.

For self-driving cars less than a Level 5, there must be a human driver present in the car. The human driver is currently considered the responsible party for the acts of the car. The AI and the human driver are co-sharing the driving task. In spite of this co-sharing, the human is supposed to remain fully immersed into the driving task and be ready at all times to perform the driving task. I've repeatedly warned about the dangers of this co-sharing arrangement and predicted it will produce many untoward results.

Let's focus herein on the true Level 5 self-driving car. Much of the comments apply to the less than Level 5 self-driving cars too, but the fully autonomous AI self-driving car will receive the most attention in this discussion.

Here's the usual steps involved in the AI driving task:

- Sensor data collection and interpretation

- Sensor fusion

- Virtual world model updating

- AI action planning

- Car controls command issuance

Another key aspect of AI self-driving cars is that they will be driving on our roadways in the midst of human driven cars too. There are some pundits of AI self-driving cars that continually refer to a utopian world in which there are only AI self-driving cars on the public roads. Currently there are about 250+ million conventional cars in the United States alone, and those cars are not going to magically disappear or become true Level 5 AI self-driving cars overnight.

Indeed, the use of human driven cars will last for many years, likely many decades, and the advent of AI self-driving cars will occur while there are still human driven cars on the roads. This is a crucial point since this means that the AI of self-driving cars needs to be able to contend with not just other AI self-driving cars, but also contend with human driven cars. It is easy to envision a simplistic and rather unrealistic world in which all AI self-driving cars are politely interacting with each other and being civil about roadway interactions. That's not what is going to be happening for the foreseeable future. AI self-driving cars and human driven cars will need to be able to cope with each other.

Returning to the topic of an olfactory sensor or e-nose for an AI self-driving car, let's consider what this sensor might consist of and how it might be utilized.

First, be aware that there is not yet an e-nose or true "machine olfactory" device in existence today.

You can today purchase a low-cost electronic sniffing device that might be devoted to a particular scent and performs a very rudimentary version of an e-nose (I wouldn't even consider it an e-nose, maybe a small part of an e-nostril, at best).

One such example would be a meter used to detect natural gas. These kinds of devices are usually handheld, meaning they are mobile, and you often need to bring to the attention of the device an odor, which it might or might not be able to register (you often have an antenna-like stick that acts as the electronic sniffer). These devices can be used by those working in the field that need to quickly gauge how much natural gas might be in the air. There are also versions that can be outfitted to be used in a manufacturing facility or in an energy plant (sometimes mobile, sometimes affixed or anchored in place).

I'm aiming to discuss herein instead a true electronic nose that could potentially detect the range of odors that a human could detect. It is said that humans are able to have around 10,000 odors that they gradually become familiar with. This is also why as you get older you tend to get less excited about odors per se, since you've potentially already detected them and mentally cataloged them. At an older age, encountering a new odor is often a rare treat and one that you ought to give some due attention to, since if you've had much of a traveled life you likely have already gotten used to most everyday odors.

Imagine a true e-nose device that is somehow part of or attached to an AI self-driving car. It is to be considered "equal" as a kind sensory partner in comparison to any other sensory device on the self-driving car. Just as the cameras have their own particular capabilities and limitations, so too would the e-nose device. Similarly, just as the cameras and radar and the rest all have specialized software that collects their data and interprets it, so too would the e-nose device.

There might be multiple e-noses associated with the AI self-driving car. You might have ones that are placed at the front and the rear of the self-driving car. Besides being outside of the AI self-driving car, there could also be e-noses inside the AI self-driving car. The number of such e-noses would partially depend upon the cost of each one, along with its size and electrical power requirements.

This brings up a point that some would argue provides reasons to not put an e-nose device onto or into an AI self-driving car. Namely, if the device or multiple such e-noses are going to be physically in or on the self-driving car, it adds weight to the self-driving car. It also chews up electrical power. The size might also mean that you need to reshape areas of the car to accommodate the devices. Will the added weight, the changes in the shaping, and the power consumption be worth whatever the e-noses devices might provide as a benefit for the AI self-driving car?

The jury is still out on that question. Admittedly, since we don't have these e-noses today, it is hard to imagine an ROI (Return on Investment) calculation that would lend itself toward concluding that yes, the e-noses would be overall handy to have on-board an AI self-driving car. Thus, even if we had the technology to do it, the value provided for an AI self-driving car might not warrant having them.

You also need to consider the AI effort related to the e-noses. Once the sensory devices do their detection, they then feed into the sensor fusion portion of the AI system. This is when the various sensors are considered in terms of trying to tie together their respective indications. Maybe the camera shows a shadowy image ahead, but it is fuzzy, meanwhile the radar indicates that there is an object there and the LIDAR likewise indicates the same. The sensor fusion tries to assess the validity of each of the sensor indications and combine them in a manner that helps with the AI driving of the car.

If we add the e-noses to the pack of available sensors to be considered, you are now increasing the effort for the sensor fusion. You are also then presumably going to need to enhance the virtual world model to be able to include indications about odors that are detected. This might include the suspected nature of the odor, the intensity, the direction and distance of the source of the odor, and so on. The AI action planning portion would then need to inspect the virtual world model and try to ascertain whether the added layer of odor information provides any indications about how to best direct the motions of the self-driving car.

Does the added effort for the AI add-up to something useful? If not, you are then further burdening the AI, and you are using up potentially needlessly the precious processing cycles and memory on-board the self-driving car. There is only so much on-board processing bandwidth available and presumably it should be devoted to the primary mission of driving the car.

We need to then consider to what use the e-nose would be put and whether it adds to the mission of being able to drive the self-driving car.

If the e-nose does not add to the overall aspects of being able to properly and safely drive the self-driving car, it does not though ergo mean that we can therefore entirely opt to not consider the e-nose devices. It could be that we might want the e-nose for purposes other than as part of the driving task, such as perhaps to just notify the human occupants of the self-driving car on an informational basis or to alert them, and not otherwise because it needs to be contributing directly to the driving task aspects.

Suppose the e-nose device detects smoke that is wafting outdoors. This could be an indicator of a nearby fire. I gave earlier the example about being in the woods and smelling smoke, but of course a fire can occur anywhere. One day I was driving through my community and smelled fire and realized that one of the homes was on fire. I was about to call the fire department but then the fire trucks came roaring into the community and I realized that someone else had already fortunately alerted them.

The AI could potentially consider whether the detection of smoke outdoors of the self-driving car was of potential concern. It would need to consider the intensity of the smoke and other factors to try and ascertain whether the smoke was of any particular danger. This might then involve changing the intended driving path or might involve conversing with the human occupants and trying to jointly decide what driving changes might be needed, if any.

The e-nose might detect the smell of gasoline. It might detect the smell of natural gas. It might detect the smell of a skunk. It might detect the smell of a bakery. These are all examples that I had mentioned earlier about using my actual human nose and could be applicable for the use of an e-nose.

There are lots of other smells that could be handy for the AI self-driving car to be aware of.

The AI self-driving car might have a library of smells that the e-nose device is familiar with. Over time, perhaps via Machine Learning (ML), the e-nose would get better at detecting a wider range of odors and also get better at determining what those odors represent. Also, via the use of the OTA (Over-The-Air) updating electronic communications with the cloud of the auto maker or tech firm that made the AI self-driving car, the e-nose could get updates and potentially leverage what other e-noses across an entire fleet of cars has gleaned.

I suppose the e-nose could be used for other larger-scale purposes, such as for environmental studies. You might ask people with AI self-driving cars to consider volunteering to use their e-nose devices to try and ascertain various odors in a particular area. The odors might be an indicator of pollutants or something else going awry in the environment.

For the use of the e-noses within an AI self-driving car, it might be able to detect if somehow deadly gases are leaking into the interior cabin of the self-driving car and do so before it reaches a killer level. It might be able to identify who is in the self-driving car by their own distinct body odors and then use this as a form of personal identification for giving commands to the self-driving car. I am sure we could all come up with other uses for the e-noses inside a car.

When I mention this idea of e-noses to AI developers that are making AI self-driving cars, they raise their arms in protest and say that they do not need another thing to worry about when it comes to sensors and sensory devices.

They've already got their hands full. Right now, the focus is to get an AI self-driving car to successfully drive down a road and not hit anyone. If an e-nose won't directly help with that focus, it is pushed down on the list of things to consider.

Indeed, you could rightfully list this as an edge problem. An edge problem is at the edge or corner of what you are otherwise trying to solve. Since we don't even have e-noses today, there is not much need to be considering what to do once they arrive, assuming they do.

For some AI developers, they are intrigued by the possibility of an e-nose. It is an as yet untapped avenue of a new kind of sensors. You could be on the ground floor of something that one day we take for granted.

Rather than the snickers and laughter that I get today when I bring up the topic of electronic noses, it could be that in some future time we will take them for granted. We'll wonder what life was like beforehand, without having an e-nose device on us all the time, perhaps your smartphones and smartwatches will have them built-in.

The e-nose could raise privacy questions.

Why should an electronic device be sniffing me?

What business is it of yours that your self-driving car has detected odors in an area?

It might be a device that has disadvantages in addition to advantages.

Perhaps the ready detection of odors could lead to some form of widespread discrimination. Who knows?

For the moment, I'll just point out again that our ability to smell is a primal sense.

Humanity and most creatures rely upon the ability to smell things. It is the last frontier for being able to replicate our biological senses into something electronic. I'd say it is worthwhile keeping our eye on progress being made.

Let's just hope that the whole thing doesn't end-up stinking.

CHAPTER 5

PERPETUAL COMPUTING AND AI SELF-DRIVING CARS

Lance B. Eliot

CHAPTER 5

PERPETUAL COMPUTING
AND AI SELF-DRIVING CARS

The store manager looked at me and said that the program I had written was going to run perpetually, and he was steamed and quite upset about it.

Back in my college days, I was a gun-for-hire in terms of a willingness to whip together off-the-cuff computer programs for anyone that needed a quick-and-dirty programmable task done, doing so to earn a few extra bucks for those large pepperoni pizzas and kegs of beer that I kept ordering. The college bookstore manager had asked me to create a program that would generate some reports for him. Without taking much time to analyze the situation, I wrote a brute force algorithm that would sort the voluminous data and produce the reports.

On a Monday morning, I had launched the program and let it fly. In that era, the amount of data involved was considered rather large since it was data for all 30,000+ students and included their classes, the books required for their classes, etc. When the bookstore manager asked me how long it would take for the program to run, I hedged and said it would take about a day. In my mind, I was thinking it was around four to eight hours to run, and so I said "a day" meaning a workday, though a day might of course also mean a 24-hour period.

The next morning, I got a call from the store manager. He told me that the program was still running and it had been "a day" since I started it. I was thankful that I hadn't said it would be four to eight hours since I would have really been off-target. I assured him that the program was going to finish soon and not to get concerned. Having done the program with little attention to any kind of debugging or testing, I hadn't even included aspects that would readily allow me to check on the progress of the code. It was pretty much a wait-and-see situation.

I went to my college classes for the day and assumed that since the bookstore manager had not tried to contact me again that the program had successfully completed and presumed that he had his desired reports. Problem solved. No need to put any added energy or thought towards that sketchy program. Sure, it had used one of the most inefficient sorting algorithms known to mankind, but hey it was running uninterruptedly and how long could it take to get the job done? By Tuesday evening, I was chowing down on more pizza and pleased with having presumably gotten the bookstore manager what he had wanted.

Wednesday morning was a real wake-up call, literally. I got a call from the bookstore manager at sunrise, which I admit was not my normal waking time in college, and he was yammering away about how my program was running and running, eating up the main computer system for the store, and still there was no sign of any reports being produced. Yikes! It had now been running non-stop for 48 hours and had not yet completed.

With great embarrassment and chagrin, I promised to head over to the computer center and dig into what was going on with the program. Looking like I had been on a drunken spree the night before (I had not!), I rushed to campus and tore into the computer center to have an under-the-hood look at the execution of my program. The good news was that it was working as intended. I was sure that it would ultimately produce the reports. The bad news was that I had not considered the runtime speed, and nor had I considered how the data was structured and nor the nature of the disk drivers that were being used, the amount of memory in RAM, etc.

It was a handy lesson about what can happen when you do sloppy programming. I vowed to not let this kind of mess happen again and that I would be more "software engineering minded" henceforth.

In case you are wondering what eventually happened, believe it or not the darned thing kept running and running, and the manager asserted that I had written a program that would run perpetually. From his viewpoint, he hadn't yet seen any results and so it was all invisible runtime and no actual visible reports. Finally, on Sunday, the program completed and produced the needed reports. It had taken nearly seven days, which the store manager pointed out that the entire earth could have been created in that length of time (depending upon your beliefs).

Anyway, this story highlights the notion of having a computer that might run perpetually. Not by accident or happenstance, but by purposeful design. It is commonly referred to as perpetual computing.

Perpetual Computing Arising

Perpetual computing. It's a new and upcoming area that we'll be all thinking about in the next several years.

Imagine a computer that could run perpetually. In fact, when you consider the matter, what is it that usually would stop a computer from running perpetually? Other than the notion that it might breakdown from wear-and-tear or exhaustion, the other factor would most likely be electrical power. A computer that runs all of the time will need electrical power all of the time. Electrical power is typically a scarce and costly resource.

I'm betting that if you have a desktop computer, it is plugged into an electrical socket and thus you rarely consider how much electrical power it needs (when it is plugged in, your computer is considered "tethered" since it is physically connected with the electrical socket). If you have a laptop, I'd wager that you do pay attention to electrical power and have found yourself scrambling to find a place to plug-in your laptop before it runs out of power. For your smartphone, you certainly have experienced the same kind of anxiety about watching how much power is left and clamoring to find a way to re-charge the battery that is in the cell phone.

Consider the world once the Internet of Things (IoT) has really taken off. There are going to be tons and tons of small IoT devices that will be attached to walls, attached to doors, attached to appliances in your home, and all over the place. Some analysts claim that by the year 2020 there will be around 200 billion IoT devices and by the year 2030 a total of perhaps 1 trillion IoT devices. This already vast trillion number could increase to 10 trillion by the year 2040.

Let's assume that most of those IoT devices are powered by a battery.

Have you ever been annoyed at having to change the batteries in your home smoke alarm? You usually only have a few of those devices in your home. Pretend that you have dozens, maybe hundreds of small-scale IoT devices in your home, all of which are powered by tiny batteries. How often will you need to be changing those batteries? It could almost become a full-time job of each day walking around your house and changing batteries. Maybe we'll christen a new job for homes and businesses that provides employment for people that will change the batteries in your IoT devices.

There must be a better way to attend to the power needs of all of these ubiquitous IoT devices.

By the way, having a vast number of IoT devices is often referred to as ubiquitous computing, meaning that it is computer related devices that are all around us and everywhere. Another way to describe this trend is to call it pervasive computing. Pervasive in this context means the same thing as ubiquitous. Don't confuse though pervasive computing with perpetual computing. Pervasive just means there are a lot of computing devices, while perpetual computing means that there are some computing devices will be able to run perpetually without stopping. Though these always-on tiny devices will hopefully be beneficial, it is important to also consider the privacy concerns that they raise, along with the security related apprehensions.

How can we provide electrical power to these ubiquitous untethered computer devices and do so without the hassle and logistical nightmare of having to walk around and change their batteries?

We might instead undertake energy harvesting.

If possible, an untethered computing device might try to scavenge energy from its surroundings. One obvious means is the use of solar energy. If the computing device is outfitted with a mini-solar panel, this might provide sufficient energy to keep the device going perpetually. You need to always consider the amount of effort required to get the energy and thus make sure that the energy harvesting is "profitable" (if it takes more energy to snatch energy, you end-up with a net negative that does you little good).

There are some promising research efforts that provide a multitude of other ways to harvest energy from the environment in which the computing device resides.

You might be able to use thermal gradients and the differences in air temperature to provide power to a computing device.

You might be able to use magnetic fields to power a computing device.

The WiFi that you are using in your home or office for making electronic communications can become a power source by having computing devices that rake in the RF waves and turn those into electrical power.

It is anticipated that via miniaturization, we'll see that IoT devices keep getting smaller and smaller in size, and are able to rely entirely on energy harvesting via nearby vibrations, sound waves, chemical reactions, light waves, motion elements, and the like. These tiny and always-on IoT devices will be so small and so prevalent that some say we will to refer to them as "smart dust."

Another consideration involves how much storage capacity the computing device has for the storage of the energy collected. Does the computing device have enough energy storage capacity to survive during times when there is insufficient energy to be harvested nearby? If the computing device has essentially no energy storage capacity, it means that it "lives" off the energy harvesting and needs to be harvesting continually and hope that there is energy there to be harvested.

The ambient energy sources might be unpredictable. Here in sunny Southern California, you would assume that any kind of solar powered device would always have plenty of sunshine to draw power from. Unfortunately, I've gone on hikes in the woods with some of my hiking gear dependent upon solar power and they've gotten depleted during a hike, regrettably due to not enough sun energy striking the solar panels to keep the units powered. I'm sure its worse in climates that don't have the kind of always-on sunshine like we do.

When you first deploy any kind of IoT device, it usually comes pre-charged up. What you don't necessarily know is how long will that initial charge last? There is an initial energy allotment when the device is first deployed and depending on how the computing device functions, it might last a long time on that initial supply or it might run out quickly.

You've maybe found out from time-to-time that when you buy a child's toy that comes with a battery included, sometimes the toy maker will include a super-cheap battery that holds almost no charge at all. This keeps down their costs in terms of what is included into the toy and allows that it will at least work the moment you get home. Pretty soon though, after taking the toy out of the box and having your child play with it, the next thing you know it has run out of power and you need to replace the cheapo batteries with more robust ones.

For some of the IoT makers, they might do the same thing. They might include a low-end super-cheap battery so that the IoT computing device works for a short while, and then it runs out. If the computing device is one that is trying to make use of perpetual computing, it would switch right away into a mode of harvesting energy and not need to dip into the initial charge, or it might be able to recharge the initial charge, doing so on its own while harvesting.

If we don't find ways to achieve perpetual computing, it implies that you might eventually end-up with IoT devices all around your home and work that are just sitting there and doing nothing at all, because they've run out of power and it is too troublesome to try and replace their batteries. That's likely a sad waste of those devices, and it also creates a clutter.

Some are especially worried that there will become a mindset of simply throwing away IoT devices that run out of power. Consider the millions and billions of IoT devices that might get discarded, fouling up our reclamation capabilities and likely polluting our waters and earth. If the IoT was able to harvest power, presumably people would be more likely to hang onto it and make use of it.

At conferences, I often discuss perpetual computing and some people seem to think that perpetual computing equates with having perpetual motion machines. Nope, that's a misnomer. I don't think anyone of a reasonable mind would consider a computing device that can run "perpetually" due to harvesting power from its environment is the same as a perpetual motion machine. A perpetual motion machine is one that once set into motion, will continue in motion, forever, and does so without adding any additional energy into it. In the case of perpetual computing, we are straight out saying that the device will be adding energy to it, doing so in at times clever ways from its environment, but nonetheless it is not a free ride akin to what a perpetual motion machine promises.

We also need to be practical and consider that eventually these computing devices are going to wear out. The word "perpetual" needs to be taken with a grain of salt. Assuming that the perpetual computing device can really always glean sufficient energy from its surroundings, one way or another that device is ultimately going to falter or fail due to some kind of mechanical breakdown. The device might last many years, but it won't last until the end of time (well, unless you are predicting the end of time is coming sooner than I hope it will!).

What does this have to do with AI self-driving cars?

At the Cybernetic AI Self-Driving Car Institute, we are developing AI software for self-driving cars. It will be interesting to see how perpetual computing comes to play regarding the advent of AI self-driving cars.

Allow me to elaborate.

I'd like to first clarify and introduce the notion that there are varying levels of AI self-driving cars. The topmost level is considered Level 5. A Level 5 self-driving car is one that is being driven by the AI and there is no human driver involved. For the design of Level 5 self-driving cars, the auto makers are even removing the gas pedal, brake pedal, and steering wheel, since those are contraptions used by human drivers. The Level 5 self-driving car is not being driven by a human and nor is there an expectation that a human driver will be present in the self-driving car. It's all on the shoulders of the AI to drive the car.

For self-driving cars less than a Level 5, there must be a human driver present in the car. The human driver is currently considered the responsible party for the acts of the car. The AI and the human driver are co-sharing the driving task. In spite of this co-sharing, the human is supposed to remain fully immersed into the driving task and be ready at all times to perform the driving task. I've repeatedly warned about the dangers of this co-sharing arrangement and predicted it will produce many untoward results.

Let's focus herein on the true Level 5 self-driving car. Much of the comments apply to the less than Level 5 self-driving cars too, but the fully autonomous AI self-driving car will receive the most attention in this discussion.

Here's the usual steps involved in the AI driving task:

- Sensor data collection and interpretation

- Sensor fusion

- Virtual world model updating

- AI action planning

- Car controls command issuance

Another key aspect of AI self-driving cars is that they will be driving on our roadways in the midst of human driven cars too. There are some pundits of AI self-driving cars that continually refer to a utopian world in which there are only AI self-driving cars on the public roads. Currently there are about 250+ million conventional cars in the United States alone, and those cars are not going to magically disappear or become true Level 5 AI self-driving cars overnight.

Indeed, the use of human driven cars will last for many years, likely many decades, and the advent of AI self-driving cars will occur while there are still human driven cars on the roads. This is a crucial point since this means that the AI of self-driving cars needs to be able to contend with not just other AI self-driving cars, but also contend with human driven cars. It is easy to envision a simplistic and rather unrealistic world in which all AI self-driving cars are politely interacting with each other and being civil about roadway interactions. That's not what is going to be happening for the foreseeable future. AI self-driving cars and human driven cars will need to be able to cope with each other.

Returning to the topic of perpetual computing, let's consider how the advent of these new innovations in energy production might impact AI self-driving cars.

First, it certainly would be tremendous if somehow the self-driving car itself could harvest energy from its surroundings, thus no longer being "tethered" to having to go to a gasoline station for a refill and nor needing to be connected to a charger for an EV (Electrical Vehicle).

One means of providing energy consists of solar panels on a self-driving car. Right now, the energy derived would be insufficient to fully run the self-driving car. You also need to take into account the size of the solar panels and their weight, which then impacts the car design and shape. As per my earlier comments, even if this could be perfected you would then still have the unpredictable nature of the solar energy that might be available and also in some parts of the world you would barely have use for this approach for most of the year.

I am not counting out the solar route and just saying that until there are more breakthroughs in terms of their size, shape, and energy harvesting capability, it is unlikely to do much for self-driving cars other than to act as a mild add-on for potentially providing some limited amount of energy generation.

Another means to gain energy would be via regenerative braking. Your car brakes can be used to convert kinetic energy into electrical power. In essence, you are recovering energy that would otherwise be tossed away by the brakes as heat. Instead, you take the friction and put it to a more useful purpose, namely helping to power the self-driving car.

Similar to the issue about the solar panels, right now the use of regenerative braking can only supply a rather small amount of electrical power. It is not going to be enough to run the self-driving car. In any case, it is something to be watched and will ultimately likely be a handy contributor to the power needs of the self-driving car.

Akin to the conversion of kinetic energy with the brakes, you can also make tires that are embedded with nanogenerators and have those specialized tires generate electrical power from the roadway friction. Right now, your tires are creating friction as they come in contact with the roadway surface, but your car is just tossing away that potential energy. Harvesting it will help provide some energy to the self-driving car, though again a rather minor amount and be insufficient to truly power-up the self-driving car.

There are lots of other ideas out there about this matter. Maybe we would have along our roadways various magnetic generator boxes that the self-driving car could grab energy from as it whooshes past the boxes on the highway. Perhaps the self-driving car could make use of temperature gradients to try and harvest energy. And so on.

For now, I'll say that you cannot hold your breath that any of these approaches will in the near-term arise sufficiently to be able to fully power an AI self-driving car. They will each be handy supplemental sources of energy, but not "the" source.

We ought to then return to the notion that perpetual computing will likely consist of very small IoT devices that have a built-in energy harvester. The energy harvest has to be tiny too, since otherwise it would bulk-up the IoT device. The weight of the energy harvester element also has be to relatively low, since it would make the IoT device hefty and heavy.

This could be handy for the sensors of the AI self-driving car.

Right now, we are assuming that the sensory devices on an AI self-driving car will all be powered by the AI self-driving car per se. Suppose though that some of the sensors could provide their own power? This would then cause less of a drain on the self-driving car and reduce its need to generate the tremendous amount of power required to run all of the sensory devices (of which their will be many included onto and into a self-driving car).

You might then more readily be able to add more sensors to the AI self-driving car too. Knowing that they can harvest their own energy means that it relieves the self-driving car of having to do so. Of course, the downside involves the chance that the sensor is not able to harvest energy when needed and the sensor goes blank, such as if the self-driving car is doing 80 miles per hour on the freeway and the sensor is supposed to be providing key readings to the AI system on-board the self-driving car but runs out of power.

One approach would be to tie the perpetual computing devices into the electrical power of the AI self-driving car, and yet only have those devices draw power from the self-driving car when they otherwise are not able to grab sufficient energy from their surroundings on their own. Indeed, you could have a two-way flow, involving the perpetual computing devices not only drawing energy from the self-driving car when needed, but also possibly pouring energy into the AI self-driving car if the device is able to grab more energy than itself needs to function.

Another aspect of self-driving cars will be the number and variety of IoT devices that are included into the self-driving car by the auto maker, along with the numerous IoT devices that passengers will bring with them into an AI self-driving car. These IoT devices might need to tap into the electrical reserves of the self-driving car to be able to run. On the other hand, if they are able to be perpetual computing devices, they might be able to harvest energy on their own and not bother using up the power of the self-driving car (plus, possibly even be able to contribute their "excess" energy to the self-driving car).

Some have speculated that perhaps via V2V (vehicle-to-vehicle communications) there will be an opportunity for self-driving cars to not only share electronic communications but also share energy. While your AI self-driving car is on the highway, it might be immersed in heavy traffic and other self-driving cars nearby are sharing roadway traffic info via V2V with your self-driving car. At the same time, it could be that the V2V allows your self-driving car to grab some of the excess energy generated via the V2V, and the energy can be plowed back into the electrical power reserves of the self-driving car.

This could likewise potentially be the case with V2I (vehicle-to-infrastructure communications). V2I consists of the roadway infrastructure sending electronic communications to your AI self-driving car. An upcoming bridge might electronically warn your self-driving car that the bridge is blocked and not usable at this time.

A street up ahead might forewarn your self-driving car that there is a big pothole in the road and it should be avoided. In the process of making those V2I communications, energy might be harvested from the excess of those communications.

Perpetual computing can be in the small and in the large. Currently, the focus is primarily on the small, mainly the IoT devices that we are going to be using in the billions and someday trillions of them. It would be a boon to society if those IoT devices could harvest their own energy and work around the clock, as needed, without having to plug them in (tether them) and nor having to replace their batteries.

Say, excuse me for a moment as I have to go change the batteries in my outdoor portable lights – which I hope soon to be able to never say again, namely, I'd like to eliminate the phrase of "go change the batteries." Let's aim for that.

.

CHAPTER 6

BYZANTINE GENERALS PROBLEM

AND

AI SELF-DRIVING CARS

Lance B. Eliot

CHAPTER 6

BYZANTINE GENERALS PROBLEM
AND
AI SELF-DRIVING CARS

The flashlight was only working intermittently.

I shook it to get the bulb to shine and cast some light. One moment the flashlight had a nice strong beam and the next moment it was faded and not of much use. At times, the light emanating from the flashlight would go on-and-off or it would dip so close to being off that I would shake it vigorously and generally the light would momentarily revive.

We were hiking in the mountains as part of our Boy Scout troop's wilderness-survival preparations and I was an adult Scoutmaster helping to make sure that none of the Scouts got hurt during the exercise. At this juncture, it was nearly midnight and the moon was providing just enough natural light that the Scouts could somewhat see the trail we were on. We had been instructed to not use flashlights since the purpose of this effort was to gauge readiness for surviving in the forests without having much in-hand other than the clothes on your back.

There were some parts of the trail that meandered rather close to a sheer cliff and I figured that adding some artificial light to the situation would be beneficial. Yes, I was tending to violate the instructions about not using a flashlight, but I was also trying to abide by the even higher directive to make sure that none of the Scouts got injured or perished during this exercise. I had taken along an older flashlight that was at the bottom of my backpack and mainly there for emergency situations. At camp, I had plenty of newer flashlights and had brought tons of batteries as part of my preparation for this trip.

While watching the Scouts as they trudged along the trail, I was mentally trying to figure out what might be wrong with the flashlight that I had been trying to use periodically during this hike. Could it be that the batteries were running low? If so, there wasn't much that I could do about it now that I was out on the trek. Or, it could be that the bulb and the internal flashlight mechanism were loose and at times disconnected, thus it would shift around as I was hiking on this rather bumpy and rutty trail. If a loose wire or connection was the problem, I could likely fix the flashlight right away, perhaps even doing so as we were in the midst of hiking.

Turns out we soon finished the hike and reached camp, and I opted to quickly replace the flashlight with one of my newer ones that worked like a charm. Problem solved.

I'm guessing that you've probably had a similar circumstance with a flashlight, wherein sometimes it wants to work and sometimes not. Of course, this kind of intermittent performance is not confined to flashlights. Various mechanical contraptions can haunt us with intermittent performance, whether it might be a flashlight, a washing machine, a hair dryer, etc.

When I was younger, I had a rather beat-up older car that was in a bit of disrepair and it seemed to have one aspect or another that would go wrong without any provocation. One moment, the engine would start and it ran fine, while at other times the car refused to start and once underway might suddenly conk out. I had taken the ill-behaving beast to a car mechanic and his advice was simple, get rid of the old car and get a new one. That didn't especially help my situation since at the time I could not afford a new car and was trying to do what I could to keep my existing car running as best as practical (with spit and bailing wire, as they say).

Let's shift for now to another topic, which you'll see relates to this notion of things that work intermittently.

When I was a university professor, I used to have my computer science students undertake an in-class exercise that was surprising to them and unexpected for a computer science course. Indeed, when I first tried the exercise, students would balk and complain that it was taking time away from focusing on learning about software development. I assured them that they would realize the value of the short effort if they just gave it a chance. I'm happy to say that not only did the students later on indicate it was worth the half hour or so of class time, it became one of the more memorable exercises out of the many of the computer science classes that they were required to take.

I would have each student pair-up with another student. It could be a fellow student that they already knew, or someone that they had not yet met in the class. Each pair would sit in a chair, facing each other across a table, and there was a barrier placed on the table that prevented them from seeing the surface of the table on the other side of the barrier.

I would give to each person a jigsaw puzzle containing about a dozen pieces. The pieces of the jigsaw puzzle were rather irregular in shape and size. The pieces also had various colors. Thus, one piece of the jigsaw puzzle might be blue and a shape that was oval, while another piece might be red and was the shape of a rectangle.

One member of each respective pair would get the jigsaw puzzle already assembled and thus "solved" in terms of being put together. The other person of the pair would get the jigsaw pieces in a bag and they were all loose and not assembled in any manner. The person with the assembled jigsaw puzzle was supposed to verbally instruct the other member of their pair to take out the pieces from the bag and assemble the puzzle. The rules included that you could not hold-up the pieces and show them to the other person, which prevented for example the person with the fully assembled jigsaw puzzle of just holding it up for the other person to see it.

You were now faced with a situation of via verbal indications only, trying to get the other person to assemble the jigsaw puzzle. This kind of exercise is often done in business schools and it is intended to highlight the nature of communications, social interaction, human behavior, and problem solving. There are plentiful lessons to be had, even though it is a rather quick and easy exercise. For anyone that hasn't done this before, it usually makes a strong impression on them.

Since the computer science students were rather cocky and felt that they could readily do such a simple exercise, they launched into the effort right away. No need to first consider how to solve this problem and instead just start talking. That's what I anticipated they might do (I had purposely refrained from offering any tips or suggestions of how to proceed), and they fell right into the trap.

A student in a given pair might say to the other one, find the red piece and put it up toward the right as it will be the upper right corner piece for the puzzle. Now, take the blue piece and put it toward the lower left as it will be the lower left corner piece. And so on. This would be similar to solving any kind of jigsaw puzzle, often starting by finding the edges and putting those into place, and then once the edge or outline is completed you might work towards the middle area assembly.

This puzzle solving approach normally would be just fine. There was a twist or trick involved in this puzzle. The assembled puzzle was not necessarily the same as the disassembled one that the other person had. In some cases, the shape of the pieces was the same and went into the same positions of the assembled puzzle, but the colors the pieces were different. Or, the shapes were different, and the colors were the same.

Here's what would happen when the students launched into the matter.

The person with the assembled puzzle would tell the other one to put the red piece in the upper right, but it turns out that the other person's red piece didn't go there and was intended to go say in the lower left corner position. Since neither of the pair could see the other person's pieces, they would not have any immediate way of realizing that they were each playing with slightly different puzzle pieces.

When the person trying to assemble their puzzle was unable to do so, it would lead to frustration for them and the person trying to instruct them, each becoming quite exasperated. Banter was quite acrid at times. I told you to put the red piece in the upper right corner, didn't you do as I told you? Yes, I put it there, but things aren't working out and it doesn't seem to go there. Well, I'm telling you that the red piece must go there. Etc.

Given that many of the computer science students were perfectionists, it made things even more frustrating for them and they were convinced that the other person was a complete dolt. The person with the dissembled pieces was sure that the other person was an idiot and could not properly explain how the puzzle was assembled. The person with the assembled pieces was sure that the other person trying to assemble the puzzle was refusing to follow instructions and was being obstinate and a jerk.

When I revealed the matter by lifting the barrier, there were some students that said the exercise was unfair. They had assumed that each of them was getting the same puzzle as the person on the other side of the barrier (I never stated this to be the case, though it certainly would seem "logical" to assume it). It was unfair, they loudly crowed, and insisted that the exercise was senseless and quite upsetting.

I asked how many of the students took the time at the start to walk through the nature of the pieces that they had in-hand. None did so. They all just jumped right away into trying to "solve the problem" of assembling the pieces. I pointed out that if they had begun by inspecting the pieces and talking with each other about what they had, it would have likely been a faster and more likely path of "solving the problem" than by just skipping straight into it.

What was interesting too is that some of the students at times were sure during the exercise that the other student was purposely trying to be difficult and possibly even lying. If you told the other student to put the red piece in the upper right corner, you had no way to know for sure that they did so. They might say they did, but you couldn't see it with your own eyes. As such, when the puzzle pieces weren't fitting together, the person giving instructions began to suspect that the other person was lying about what they were doing.

There were some students that even thought that perhaps I had arranged with the member of the pair to intentionally lie during the exercise. It was as though I had somehow before class started been able to reach half of the class secretly and tell them to make things difficult during the puzzle exercise and lie to the other person. Amazingly, even pairs of friends thought the same thing. Quite a conspiracy theory!

Tying this tale of the puzzle solving to my earlier story about the intermittent flashlight, the crux is that you might find yourself sometimes immersed into a system that has aspects that are not working as you imagined they would. Is this because those other elements are purposefully doing so, or is it by happenstance? In whatever manner it is occurring, what can you do to rectify the situation? Are you even ready in case a system that you are immersed into might suddenly begin to have such difficulties?

Welcome to the Byzantine Generals Problem.

First introduced in a 1982 paper that appeared in the ACM Transactions on Programming Languages and Systems, aptly entitled "The Byzantine Generals Problem," there are numerous variants of the now-classic problem and what to do about it. It is a commonly described and taught problem in computer science classes and covers an important topic that anyone involved especially in real-time systems development should be aware of.

It has to do with fault-tolerance. You might have a system that contains elements or sub-components that might at one point or another suffer a fault. Upon having a fault, the element or sub-component might not make life so easy that the element or sub-component just outright fails and stops.

In a sense, if an element stops completely from working, you are in an "easier" diagnostic situation in that you can perhaps declare that element or sub-component "dead" and no longer usable, versus the more torturous route of having an element or sub-component that kind of works but not entirely so.

What can be particularly trying is a situation of an element or sub-component that intermittently works. In that case, you need to figure out how to handle something that might or might not work when you need it to work. If my flashlight had not worked at all, I would have assumed that the batteries were dead or that the wiring was bad, and I would not have toyed with the flashlight at all, figuring it was beyond hope. But, since the flashlight was nearly working, I was hopeful of trying to deal with the faults and see what could be done.

You could of course declare outright that any element or sub-component that falters is considered "dead" and therefore you will henceforth pretend that it is. In the case of my flashlight, due to the intermittent nature of it, I might have just put it back into my backpack and decide that it was not worth playing around with it. Sure, it did still kind of work, but I might decide to declare it dead and finished.

The downside there is that I've then given up on something that still has some life to it, and therefore some practical value. Plus, there is an outside chance that it might opt to start working correctly, doing so all of the time and no longer be intermittent. And, there's a chance that I might be able to play with it and get it to work properly, even if it won't happen to do so of its own accord.

For the flashlight, I wasn't sure what was the source of the underlying problem. Was it the batteries? Was it the wiring? Was it the bulb? This can be another difficulty associated with faults in a system. You might not know or readily be able to discern where the fault exists. You might know that overall the system isn't working as intended, but the specific element or sub-component that is causing the trouble might be hidden or buried within lots of other elements or sub-components.

With my fussy car that I had when I was younger, if the engine wouldn't start, I had no ready means of knowing where the fault was. I took in the car and the mechanic changed the starter. This seemed to help and the car ran for about a week. It then refused to start again. I took the car to the auto mechanic a second time and this time he changed the spark plugs. This helped for a few days. Unfortunately, infuriatingly, it stopped running again. Inch by inch, I was being tortured by elements of the car that would experience a fault (in this case, fatal faults rather than intermittent ones).

One fault can at times intermingle with another fault. This makes things doubly challenging.

It's usually easiest (and often naïve) to think that you can find "the one" element that is causing the difficulty and then deal with that element only. In real life, it is often the case that you end-up with several elements or sub-components at fault. If the starter for my car is intermittently working, and also if my spark plugs are intermittently working, it can be dizzying and maddening since they might function or not function in a wide variety of combinatorial circumstances. Just when I think the problem is the starter, it works fine, and yet maybe then the car still won't start. When I then think that the problem is the spark plugs, maybe it starts but then later it doesn't due to the bad starter.

You can have what are considered "error avalanches" that cascade through a system and are due to one or more elements or sub-components that are suffering faults.

Remember too that a fault does not imply that the element or sub-component won't work at all. The faulty element can do its function in a half-baked way. If the batteries in the flashlight were low on energy, they were perhaps only able to provide enough of a charge to light the flashlight part of the time. They apparently weren't completely depleted of their charge, since the flashlight was at least still partially able to light-up.

A fault can be even more inadvertently devious in that it might not function in a half-baked way and instead provide false or misleading aspects, not necessarily because it is purposely trying to lie to you. The students that were telling each other which piece to use for the puzzle were genuinely trying to express what to do. None of them were purposely trying to lie and get the other person confused. They were each being truthful as best they presumed in the circumstance.

I am not ruling out that an element or sub-component might intentionally lie, and merely emphasizing that the fault in an element or sub-component can cause it to lie, and this might be "lying" without such intent or indeed it might be that the element or sub-component is purposely lying.

A student in the puzzle exercise could have intentionally chosen to lie, which maybe the person might do to get the other person upset. I've known some professors that tried this tactic as a variant to the puzzle solving problem, infusing the added complication of truth or lies detection into it. The professor would offer points to the students to purposely distort or "lie" about the puzzle assembly, and the other student needed to try and ferret out what was the truth versus what was a lie (you've perhaps seen something similar via Jimmy Fallon's popular skits involving lying versus telling the truth with celebrities that he has on his nighttime talk show).

Byzantine Fault Tolerance (BFT) is the notion that you need to design a system to be able to contend with so-called Byzantine faults, which consists of faults that might or might not involve an element or sub-component entirely going dead (known as fail-stop), and for which the fault could allow that element or sub-component to still function but in a half-baked way, or it might do worse and actually "lie" or distort whatever it is supposed to do. And, this can occur to any of the elements or sub-components, at any time, and intermittently, and can occur to only one element or sub-component at a time or might encompass multiple elements or sub-components that are each twinkling as to properly functioning.

Why is this known as the Byzantine Generals Problem? In the original 1982 setup of this intriguing "thought experiment" problem, the researchers proposed that you might have military generals in the Byzantine army that are trying to take a city or fort. Suppose that the generals will need to coordinate their attack and will be coming at the city or fort from different angles. The timing of the attack has to be done just right. They need to attack at the same time to effectively win the battle.

We'll pretend that the generals can only communicate a simplistic message that says either to attack or to retreat. If you were a general, you would wait to see what the other generals have to say. If they are saying to attack, you would presumably attack too. If they say to retreat, you would presumably retreat too. The generals are not able to directly communicate with each other (because they didn't have cell phones in those day, ha!), and instead they use their respective lieutenants to pass messages among the generals.

You can likely guess that the generals are our elements or sub-components of a system, and we can consider the lieutenants to be elements too, though one way to treat the lieutenants in this allegory is as messengers rather than purely as traditional elements of the system. I don't want to make this too messy and long here, so I'll keep things simpler. One aspect though to keep in mind is that a fault might occur not just in the functional items of interest, but it might also occur in the communicating of their efforts. The starter in my car might work perfectly and it is only the wire that connects it to the rest of the engine that has the fault (it's the messenger that is at fault). That kind of thing.

Suppose that one or more of the generals is a traitor. To undermine the attack, the traitorous general(s) might send an attack message to some of the generals and simultaneously send a retreat message to others. This could then induce some of the generals into attacking and yet they might not be sufficient in numbers to win and take the city or fort. Those generals attacking might get wiped out. The loyal generals would be considered non-faulty, and the traitorous generals would be considered "faults" in terms of how they are functioning.

There are all kinds of proposed solutions to dealing with the Byzantine Generals Problem.

You can mathematically describe the situation and then try to show a mathematical solution, along with providing handy rules-of-thumb about it. For example, depending upon how you describe and restrict the nature of the problem, you could say that in certain situations as long as only a third or less of the participants are traitors you can provide a method to deal with the traitorous acts (this comes from a mathematical formulation of $n > 3t$, wherein t is the number of traitors and n is the number of generals).

I use the Byzantine Generals Problem to bring up the broader notion of Byzantine Fault Tolerance, namely that anyone involved in the design and development of a real-time system needs to be planning for the emergence of faults within the real-time system, beyond just assuming they will encounter "dead" or fail-stop faults, and must design and develop the real-time system to cope with faults of an intermittent nature and faults that can at times tell the truth or lie.

What does this have to do with AI self-driving cars?

At the Cybernetic AI Self-Driving Car Institute, we are developing AI software for self-driving cars. The AI for a self-driving car is a real-time system and has hundreds upon hundreds if not thousands of elements or sub-components.

The auto makers and tech firms crafting such complex real-time systems need to make sure they are properly taking into account the nature of Byzantine Fault Tolerance.

Bluntly, an AI self-driving car is a real-time system that involves life-or-death matters and must be able to contend with faults of a wide variety and that can happen at the worst of times. Keep in mind that an AI self-driving car could ram into a wall or crash into another car, any of which might happen because the AI system itself suffered an internal fault and the fault-tolerance was insufficient to safely keep the self-driving car from getting into a wreck.

I'd like to clarify and introduce the notion that there are varying levels of AI self-driving cars. The topmost level is considered Level 5. A Level 5 self-driving car is one that is being driven by the AI and there is no human driver involved. For the design of Level 5 self-driving cars, the auto makers are even removing the gas pedal, brake pedal, and steering wheel, since those are contraptions used by human drivers. The Level 5 self-driving car is not being driven by a human and nor is there an expectation that a human driver will be present in the self-driving car. It's all on the shoulders of the AI to drive the car.

For self-driving cars less than a Level 5, there must be a human driver present in the car. The human driver is currently considered the responsible party for the acts of the car. The AI and the human driver are co-sharing the driving task. In spite of this co-sharing, the human is supposed to remain fully immersed into the driving task and be ready at all times to perform the driving task. I've repeatedly warned about the dangers of this co-sharing arrangement and predicted it will produce many untoward results.

Let's focus herein on the true Level 5 self-driving car. Much of the comments apply to the less than Level 5 self-driving cars too, but the fully autonomous AI self-driving car will receive the most attention in this discussion.

Here's the usual steps involved in the AI driving task:

- Sensor data collection and interpretation

- Sensor fusion

- Virtual world model updating

- AI action planning

- Car controls command issuance

Another key aspect of AI self-driving cars is that they will be driving on our roadways in the midst of human driven cars too. There are some pundits of AI self-driving cars that continually refer to a utopian world in which there are only AI self-driving cars on the public roads. Currently there are about 250+ million conventional cars in the United States alone, and those cars are not going to magically disappear or become true Level 5 AI self-driving cars overnight.

Indeed, the use of human driven cars will last for many years, likely many decades, and the advent of AI self-driving cars will occur while there are still human driven cars on the roads. This is a crucial point since this means that the AI of self-driving cars needs to be able to contend with not just other AI self-driving cars, but also contend with human driven cars.

It is easy to envision a simplistic and rather unrealistic world in which all AI self-driving cars are politely interacting with each other and being civil about roadway interactions. That's not what is going to be happening for the foreseeable future. AI self-driving cars and human driven cars will need to be able to cope with each other.

Returning to the Byzantine Fault Tolerance matter, let's consider the various aspects of an AI self-driving car and how it needs to be designed and developed to contend with a myriad of potential faults.

Let's start with the sensors.

An AI self-driving car has numerous sensors, including cameras, radar, ultrasonic, LIDAR, and other sensory devices. Any of those sensors can experience a fault. The fault might involve the sensor going "dead" and into a fault-stop state. Or, the fault might cause the sensor to report only partial data or only a partial interpretation of the data collected by the sensor. Worse still, the fault could encompass that the sensor is "lying" about the data or its interpretation of the data.

When I use the word "lying" it is not intended herein to imply necessarily that someone has been traitorous and gotten the sensor to purposely lie about what data it has or the interpretation of the data. I'm herein instead suggesting that the sensor might provide false data that doesn't exist, or provide real data that has been changed to falsely represent the original data, or provided an interpretation of the data that maybe originally would have said one thing but instead gave something completely contrary. This could occur by happenstance due to the nature of the fault.

Those could also of course be purposeful and intentional "lies" in that suppose a nefarious person has hacked into the AI self-driving car and forced the sensors to internally tell falsehoods.

Or, maybe the bad-hat hacker has planted a computer virus that causes the sensors to tell falsehoods. The virus might not even be forcing the sensors to do so and instead be working as a man-in-the-middle attack that takes whatever the sensors report, blocks the messages, substitutes its own messages of a contrary nature, and sends them along. It could be that the AI self-driving car has been attacked by an outsider, or it could be that even an insider that aided the development of the AI self-driving car had implanted a virus that would at some future time become engaged.

Overall, the AI needs to protect itself from itself.

The AI developers should have considered beforehand the potential for faults occurring with the various elements and sub-components of the AI system. There then should have been numerous checks-and-balances included within the AI system to try and detect the faults. Besides detecting the faults, there need to be systematic ways in which the faults are then dealt with.

In the case of the sensors, pretend that one of the cameras is experiencing a fault. The camera is still partially functioning. It is not entirely "dead" or at a fail-stop status. The images are filled with noise and it makes the images occluded or confused looking. The internal system software that deals with this particular camera does not realize that the camera is having troubles. The troubles come and go, meaning that at one moment the camera is providing pristine and accurate images, while the next moment it does not.

We've previously let's say put in place a Machine Learning (ML) component that has been trained to be able to detect pedestrians. After having scrutinized thousands and thousands of street scenes with pedestrians, the Machine Learning algorithm using an Artificial Neural Network has gotten pretty good at picking out the shape of a pedestrian in even crowded street scenes. It does so with a rather high reliability.

The Machine Learning component gets fed a lousy camera image that has been populated with lots of static and noise, due to the subtle fault in the camera. This has made the portion that has a pedestrian in it very hazy and fuzzy, and the ML is unable to detect a pedestrian to any significant probability. The ML reports this to the sensor fusion portion of the AI system.

We now have a situation wherein a pedestrian exists in the street ahead of us, but the interpretation of the camera scene has indicated there is not a pedestrian there. Is the Machine Learning component lying? In this case, it has done its genuine job and concluded that there is not a pedestrian there. I suppose we would say it is not lying per se. If it had been implanted with a computer virus that caused it to intentionally ignore the presence of a pedestrian and misreport as such to the rest of the AI, we might then consider that to be a lie.

One should be asking why the system element that drives the camera has not yet detected that the camera has a fault? Furthermore, we might expect the ML element to be suspicious of images that have static and noise, though of course that could be happening a lot of the time in a more natural manner that has nothing to do with faults. Presumably, once the interpretation reaches the sensor fusion portion of the AI system, the sensor fusion will try to triangulate the accuracy and "honesty" of the interpretation by comparing to the other sensors, including other cameras, the radar, the LIDAR, and the like.

You could liken the various sensors to the generals in the Byzantine Generals Problem.

The sensor fusion must try to ferret out which of the generals (the sensors) are being truthful and which are not, though it is not quite so straightforward as a simple attack versus retreat kind of message. Instead, the matter is much more complex involving where objects are in the surrounding area and whether those objects are near to the AI self-driving car, or whether they pose a threat to the self-driving car, or whether the self-driving car poses a threat to them. And so on.

The sensor fusion then reports to the virtual world model update component of the AI system. The virtual world model updater code would place a maker in the virtual world as to where the pedestrian is standing, though if the sensors misreported the presence of the pedestrian and the sensor fusion did not catch the fault, the virtual world model would now mispresent the world around it. The AI action planner would then not realize a pedestrian is nearby.

The AI action planner might not issue car controls commands to maneuver the car away from the pedestrian.

The pedestrian might get runover by the AI self-driving car, all stemming from a subtle fault in a camera. This is a fault that had the AI system been better designed and constructed it should have been able to catch. There should have been other means established to deal with a potentially faulty sensor.

I had mentioned earlier to avoid falling into the mental trap of assuming that there will be just one fault at a time.

Recall that my old car had the starter that seemed to come-and-go and also the spark plugs that were working intermittently, thus, there were really two items at fault, each of which reared its ugly head from time-to-time (though not necessarily at the same time).

Suppose a camera on an AI self-driving car experiences a subtle fault, which is intermittent.

Imagine that the sensor fusion component of the AI software also has a fault, a subtle one, occurring from time-to-time. These two might arise completely separately of each other.

They might also happen to arise at the same time. The AI system needs to be shaped in a manner that it can handle multiple faults from multiple elements, across the full range of elements and subcomponents, and for which those faults occur in subtle ways at varying times.

Conclusion

The tale of the Byzantine Generals Problem is helpful to serve as a reminder that modern day real-time systems need to be built with fault tolerance.

There are some AI developers that came from a university or research lab that might not have been particularly concerned with fault tolerance since they were devising experimental systems to explore new advances in AI.

When shifting such AI systems into everyday use, it is crucial that fault tolerance be baked into the very fabric of the AI system.

We are going to have the emergence of AI self-driving cars that will be on our streets and will be operating fully unattended by a human driver. W

e rightfully should expect that fault tolerance has been given a top priority for these real-time systems that are controlling multi-ton vehicles. Without proper and appropriate fault tolerance, the AI self-driving car you see coming down the street could go astray due to a subtle fault in some hidden area of the AI.

An error avalanche could allow the fault to cascade to a level that the AI self-driving car then gets into an untoward incident and human lives are jeopardized.

One of the greatest emperors of the Byzantines was Justinian I, and it is claimed that he had said that safety of the state was the highest law.

For those AI developers involved in designing and building AI self-driving car systems, I hope that you will abide by Justinian's advice and aim to ensure that you have dutifully included Byzantine Fault Tolerance or the equivalent thereof for aiming to have safety as the highest attention in your AI system. Consider that an order by Roman Law, per the Codex Justinianus.

CHAPTER 7

DRIVER TRAFFIC GUARDIANS

AND

AI SELF-DRIVING CARS

Lance B. Eliot

CHAPTER 7

DRIVER TRAFFIC GUARDIANS
AND
AI SELF-DRIVING CARS

The holiday season traffic can be difficult to navigate.

I had just gotten done doing some shopping at a popular mall and was pulling out of the mall parking lot, trying to enter into traffic onto a rather busy street that had lots of cars zipping along. Though you might think that people would be in a good mood because the holidays were just around the corner, it seemed that most drivers were crazed and driving as though it was their last day on Earth. Drivers were snarling at each other, cutting each other off, and otherwise driving as if it were a dog-eat-dog occasion.

Suddenly, a car came to a stop just before the mall exit that I was waiting at and offered to let me into the stream of traffic. I assumed at first that the driver was probably trying to come into the mall at this juncture and so was letting me go first, getting my car out of the way, so that they could then come into the mall.

But, the driver didn't have a turn signal on, which would have indicated they were going to turn into the mall. Furthermore, I knew this was considered an exit from the mall and though you could drive into the exit area, it tended to make for confusion of drivers in the mall that were usually all jockeying at the exit to get out of the mall.

I smiled at the driver and did a quick wave with my hand, suggesting that they should go ahead and continue forward on the street and not continue to hold-up traffic behind them.

I also did a bit of a head shake and a hand movement warning that this was not a proper and safe means to enter into the mall. I hoped that my gestures would be taken in a positive manner. I was trying to help out this other driver. I figured too that perhaps the driver was trying to help me by holding back traffic, doing so was a quite kind and thought act, and I thought that my waving and head nodding might be a quid-pro-quo in return (aiding them by warning that coming into the exit area might be dangerous for them and I was thoughtfully considering their safety).

The driver of the car made no particular head motion or arm waving in return. Meanwhile, the driver kept their car in this holding position. I could see that the eyes of the driver were turned in my direction and it seemed hard to believe that they had not seen my waving and head gestures to them. Just in case, I rolled down my window and put my arm outside, and did a large waving motion to make it abundantly clear that they should move ahead and not continue to keep the street blocked.

I was somewhat leery though of prolonging the matter. First, it could erupt into road rage. The driver that was holding back the traffic might misinterpret my gestures and think that I am perhaps holding up the middle finger as though I am insulting them. The traffic behind me was getting exasperated because they wanted to get out of the mall parking lot and could see that I had an opportunity to move forward. They probably were having rather foul thoughts about me. Why wasn't that dolt pulling out into the street?

You might even be wondering why I would not go ahead and pull out into the street, taking advantage of the car that was holding back traffic. I suppose that I could have done so, and there have been times that I have made use of such a situation to proceed ahead. In this case, my main hesitation was twofold.

My first point of hesitation was that the driver that was holding back traffic did not look particularly trustworthy to me. This is a judgement call, I realize. I was somehow slightly suspicious that I might go ahead forward into traffic and the driver might suddenly speed-up. I've seen this happen before. A driver that was intending to hold back traffic suddenly opts to not do so, and moves forward unexpectedly, catching the other driver off-guard and it can at times lead to confusion and worse still a car accident.

My second point of hesitation was that the traffic on this particular street was moving along at a fast clip and there was a tremendous volume of traffic. As such, some cars were opting to go past the stopped driver and then cut into the lane that the driver was blocking. If I went into the spot that the driver was blocking for me to get into the street, there was also a chance that another car might go around that driver and then try to whip into "my" lane at that moment, and we'd end-up in a potential collision.

All in all, I was willing to let the driver proceed and wait for a moment when the traffic had slowed down sufficient that I could snake my way into the lane. I didn't really want someone holding up traffic for me. It was a presumably kind gesture to do so, but it actually was making the situation dicey. They probably had no clue as to why I was hesitating and just assumed that I was unaware of what a nice gesture was being offered to me. I doubt the driver had contemplated and calculated the risks involved in this maneuver.

I'm guessing that you've likely had similar kinds of driving circumstances. Another driver opts to try and do something for you that allows you to get your car into traffic, and you need to decide whether to proceed or not. The other driver is actually ceding the right-of-way to you.

Of course, it is questionable whether a driver can cede the right-of-way in this manner. If you were to get into a car accident due to taking the right-of-way baton, I'd bet that by-and-large you'd be held responsible. The judge would certainly want to know who had the legal right-of-way, and though it was perhaps nice that another driver seemed to grant you the informal right-of-way, strictly speaking the rules-of-the-road would be against you since you had illegally "failed to yield the right-of-way" (in spite of your claim and clamoring that the right-of-way had been presumably handed to you).

I've seen novice teenage drivers fall for a kind of right-of-way ceding trap. These novice drivers are just learning how to best navigate the streets safely. They often assume that the more seasoned drivers on the road know what they are doing. I don't make that assumption. I'd readily claim that there are many seasoned drivers that are rather clueless about driving and make all sorts of judgement mistakes as they drive (hence too the massive number of car accidents and fender benders).

A driver that appears to grant you the right-of-way might opt to suddenly retract the offer and catch you midstream trying to take the right-of-way. Or, other drivers that don't realize what is happening might make moves that end-up clobbering you and/or the right-of-way granting driver. There can also be pedestrians that can get dragged into the matter too. If there are nearby pedestrians, they might also be making predictions about what is going to happen next and become befuddled when the situation does not necessarily playout as it might seem to be.

There are also traffic downstream issues that can arise. I've often noticed that cars that are further back from the stoppage point are at times caught unawares that traffic has stopped for seemingly no valid reason.

In this case of the mall exit, there was a nearby intersection that had a green light. The cars coming down the street could see that the light was green. There would have been no expectation that traffic would come to a halt. Cars at the end of the pack that weren't paying close attention could have rammed into a car that was also at the back of the pack, simply because they had expected traffic to be zipping along and had no presence-of-mind to look ahead and realize that traffic had come to a stop.

A novice driver tends to consider these situations to be a godsend. They are happy to have someone block traffic for them and not have to on-their-own figure out how to make their way into a busy street. These naïve drivers are bound to suggest that they do not want to look a gift horse in the mouth. If some other driver is willing to grant them right-of-way, well, whether a generous gesture or maybe because the other driver is confused, it doesn't matter "why" and instead just go ahead and take the opportunity. No need to think about it.

I'm sure that some might have considered me to be a scared mouse that was too timid a driver to realize the moment existed for me to take advantage of it. As mentioned, I've indeed used these moments on some occasions, but I don't think it is a wise driver that always and automatically will use the largesse of another driver. You need to assess each such circumstance and decide whether it is a safe gamble or not.

If you've ever tried to turn down the offer from a traffic "guardian" such as my mall exit situation, you know that sometimes the guardian driver is insistent that you take their offer. The driver often assumes that for sure you need to take their offer. It even becomes a kind of game of insistence. Even though I was waving on the driver, he was still sitting there and seemingly ignoring my gestures to move along. The moment can be one of wills. The guardian driver won't back down from their offer. The other driver won't back down from not taking the offer. Both cars then are a standstill, like gun slingers facing off in the wild west.

One time, this happened to such a severity that the cars behind the guardian driver began to honk their horns, and the cars behind the driver that was not taking the opening were honking their horns too. It was a horn orchestra. This seemed to actually make the two confronting drivers even more intractable. Invariably, one of the two drivers will give in and traffic will flow again, but it will have not been without a great deal of stress and consternation all around.

Seasoned drivers will frequently make judgements about these situations and do so without much conscious thought that they are indeed mulling it over. If you've encountered these moments before, you by now have formulated an unspoken mental method to gauge the efficacy of the circumstance. Without any noticeable hesitation, you'll likely instantly opt to either take the right-of-way that was provided by the guardian or you will turn it down. You instinctively come to know what smells right and what stinks. If the situation seems to have a potential stench to it, such as bordering on your own safety driving threshold, you'll likely try to find a means to get out of it.

I don't want you to get this situation confounded with other situations that are not quite the same, even though they might seem to be the same. For example, suppose I had already started to move my car ahead into the street, prior to the guardian driver coming up to the spot where the mall exit was. If I was already protruding into the street, it could be that I was then blocking their lane and it was safest for the other driver to come to a stop. Or, even if I wasn't actually partially into the lane, if it appeared that I was intending to do so, such as my car was moving forward actively, it could also spur the other driver to come to a halt.

I've done this same thing many times in terms of noticing a car that was coming out into the street and seemingly not realizing that traffic is already coming down the street. I've had to come to a stop to let the intruder into traffic, otherwise the odds were that the driver was going to get clobbered by me or some other car. These are drivers that don't judge well the traffic situation at-hand. They have made a blunder by moving into the street prematurely.

When I say it is a blunder, that's actually a bit of an understatement. There are some drivers that are living in their own driving world and don't care about other cars. These drivers will take the right-of-way whether it is legal or not.

For them, they are all important. If they want into the street, of course all other traffic should come to a halt. They don't calculate whether other cars might need to dangerously come to a sudden halt. All that they know is that they want to get to wherever they are going, and by heck or high water they will do so.

If you are wondering what happened in my case of the mall exit, I waited to see what the guardian driver was going to do and he finally gave-up and proceeded forward. The whole matter took only a few seconds of time and my having walked you through it step-by-step might seem like it took an eternity. It is like trying to analyze a football game play that involved the quarterback tossing a pass and via a rewind you inspect the player movements step-by-step. The play itself might have taken just a few seconds but the analysis might take several minutes of careful inspection.

My mall exit example is merely one exemplar of these kinds of traffic guardian moments. There are lots of driving situations involving a driver that decides to become a traffic guardian. They take on the role of directing traffic. In some cases, their efforts are laudable. In other instances, their efforts are misguided. I'd like to think that most of the time the driver is acting in a self-less manner and genuinely wanting to help other drivers. Either way, whether the driver traffic guardian has heavenly motives or perhaps less than lofty motives, it is a driving circumstance that other drivers need to be watching for and be able to contend with.

Another example that illustrates how dangerous these driver guardian moments can become involves the other day when I was driving down a busy street that had a median dividing the traffic. It turns out that a pedestrian was standing on the median and hopeful of crossing the traffic lanes. They were doing so in a jaywalking manner. In other words, the pedestrian was not crossing at a valid crosswalk. Clearly the pedestrian was in the wrong and was potentially creating a dangerous situation for the cars streaming down the street and for them self.

Most of the cars were moving along and ignoring the pedestrian. This seemed like the prudent action for the cars. All of a sudden, one car that was closest to the median decided to come to a stop. This was completely contrary to the existing flow of traffic. There was no reason to come to a halt. Apparently, the driver noticed the "stranded" pedestrian and decided to go ahead and make their lane available for the pedestrian to cross.

Unfortunately, the lane to the right was still open and traffic was moving at a fast speed. The traffic in this still moving lane could not readily see the pedestrian. Turns out the car that had stopped in the other lane to let the pedestrian pass was a large car and it pretty much hid the pedestrian from view. So, you now had traffic zipping along in the lane that the pedestrian would next need to use to get across the street, and the traffic in that lane had no idea why the other lane had come to a halt.

I'd guess that most of the time we might assume that the stopped car had car troubles. Perhaps the stopped car had a stalled engine. Maybe there was debris on the ground in that lane so the car came to a halt. Who knows? All the drivers in the other lane that were streaming along didn't seem to care and just kept going. Meanwhile, the pedestrian had stepped into the street in front of the stopped car, and thus the stopped car no longer had any other viable option other than to remain stopped.

If the pedestrian tried to cross that remaining lane, it was going to be a really dicey effort. Cars were not expecting to see a pedestrian miraculously appear in the lane. The pedestrian might also misjudge a momentary gap in traffic and try to run across the lane to the sidewalk, but then get plowed over by a fast moving car that had no idea that the pedestrian was wanting to move across the lane. Imagine if the pedestrian leapt into the lane, and an upcoming car tried to brake, but the car slides into the pedestrian, injuring or killing them, and maybe at the same time the swerving car hits other nearby cars.

The whole cascading nightmare could have been triggered by the driver guardian that opted to come to a halt in the middle of traffic. You might say that the pedestrian is at fault for being on the median and looking like they wanted to cross the street. I'd wager that in spite of the pedestrian being in the wrong place at the wrong time, most traffic courts and traffic judges would come down hard on the driver that decided to be the traffic guardian. No matter whether the traffic guardian was trying to right the situation and be helpful, if they create a hazardous traffic situation it is their doing.

What does this have to do with AI self-driving cars?

At the Cybernetic AI Self-Driving Car Institute, we are developing AI software for self-driving cars. One aspect for the AI is that it needs to be able to contend with driver traffic guardians.

Allow me to elaborate.

I'd like to first clarify and introduce the notion that there are varying levels of AI self-driving cars. The topmost level is considered Level 5. A Level 5 self-driving car is one that is being driven by the AI and there is no human driver involved. For the design of Level 5 self-driving cars, the auto makers are even removing the gas pedal, brake pedal, and steering wheel, since those are contraptions used by human drivers. The Level 5 self-driving car is not being driven by a human and nor is there an expectation that a human driver will be present in the self-driving car. It's all on the shoulders of the AI to drive the car.

For self-driving cars less than a Level 5, there must be a human driver present in the car. The human driver is currently considered the responsible party for the acts of the car. The AI and the human driver are co-sharing the driving task. In spite of this co-sharing, the human is supposed to remain fully immersed into the driving task and be ready at all times to perform the driving task. I've repeatedly warned about the dangers of this co-sharing arrangement and predicted it will produce many untoward results.

Let's focus herein on the true Level 5 self-driving car. Much of the comments apply to the less than Level 5 self-driving cars too, but the fully autonomous AI self-driving car will receive the most attention in this discussion.

Here's the usual steps involved in the AI driving task:

- Sensor data collection and interpretation
- Sensor fusion
- Virtual world model updating
- AI action planning
- Car controls command issuance

Another key aspect of AI self-driving cars is that they will be driving on our roadways in the midst of human driven cars too. There are some pundits of AI self-driving cars that continually refer to a utopian world in which there are only AI self-driving cars on the public roads. Currently there are about 250+ million conventional cars in the United States alone, and those cars are not going to magically disappear or become true Level 5 AI self-driving cars overnight.

Indeed, the use of human driven cars will last for many years, likely many decades, and the advent of AI self-driving cars will occur while there are still human driven cars on the roads. This is a crucial point since this means that the AI of self-driving cars needs to be able to contend with not just other AI self-driving cars, but also contend with human driven cars. It is easy to envision a simplistic and rather unrealistic world in which all AI self-driving cars are politely interacting with each other and being civil about roadway interactions. That's not what is going to be happening for the foreseeable future. AI self-driving cars and human driven cars will need to be able to cope with each other.

Returning to the matter of the driver traffic guardians, let's consider how these kinds of drivers and driving situations can impact the AI of a self-driving car.

Some AI developers might say that they don't need to figure out whether someone is a driver traffic guardian. All the AI needs to do is react to whatever driving situation happens to arise. I consider this rather narrow thinking on the part of the AI developers and I assert it puts the AI itself into a (at best) novice teenage driver mindset, meaning that the chances of a car accident and the danger of injury or killing humans is going to go up if the AI cannot realize what is happening.

Let's take the mall exit example. What would the AI do? You might suggest that since the AI was intending to leave the mall, and if the stopped traffic allows for the AI self-driving car to get out of the mall, it should go ahead and proceed. No fuss, no particular complexity involved.

Suppose though that the other traffic in the street opts to suddenly swerve over into the stopped lane and collides with the AI self-driving car as it enters into the stopped lane? I'm sure that some AI developers would claim that's the fault of those other drivers and the AI was "in the right" and thus nothing else matters. But, if the AI allows the self-driving car to get into a situation for which the odds of a collision happening is relatively high, wouldn't we all agree that this is something the AI ought to be trying to anticipate? I would say so.

There are AI developers that cling to the notion that as long as the "fault" is on the heads of the other drivers, it somehow means that it is Okay for the AI to make rather short shrift decisions that get the AI self-driving car into bad or even dire circumstances. These AI developers also want to have the rest of the world accommodate the arrival of AI self-driving cars. They want other drivers to provide a wide berth for an AI self-driving car. They want other drivers and even pedestrians to tiptoe around a self-driving car when it comes down the street.

That's not the real-world. If AI self-driving cars are going to be on our real-world streets, you cannot somehow expect that the rest of the world is going to gingerly and respectively give AI self-driving cars their own special safety cushion.

Rather than trying to change the rest of the world to accommodate AI self-driving cars, I emphasize that the AI self-driving cars need to be able to be designed and built to fit to the nature of the real-world. Let's not put things upside down wherein the world has to make new roads, new rules, etc., just on behalf of AI self-driving cars.

I've previously discussed the so-called pedestrian on a pogo stick problem. This is a situation involving a human that happens to be on a pogo stick and opts to pogo into lanes of traffic. There are some AI developers that indicate that this is a ridiculous idea and would never happen. That's the first wrong answer. It could certainly happen. Secondly, the AI developers say that if it did happen, the pogoing person is clearly at fault and thus if the AI self-driving car hits the person, no big deal in the sense that it was the stupid human that led to the incident. That's another wrong answer. The AI should be able to respond to situations as they emerge.

Believe it or not, some AI developers would even say that if we are going to have pogoing humans onto roadways, the world should put up barriers to prevent any humans from getting into the roadway wherever an AI self-driving car is going to be. Can you imagine the astronomical costs of putting up barriers all across the country for this purpose? Ridiculous.

Overall, I would argue that the AI needs to be able to contend with the driving traffic guardian.

The first element of the AI involves it being able to detect that a driving traffic guardian aspect is arising. Detection is key. Once the matter is detected, the rest involves prediction of what might happen and being able to prepare an AI action plan to deal with the matter.

In the case of the mall exit, the AI via its sensors would have likely been able to detect that the car in the traffic lane had come to a stop. The question arises or should arise as to why has the car stopped there? If the traffic was flowing unabated, and if there is nothing apparent in the front of the stopped car, what else might account for the car having come to a stop?

If the AI can rule out most other relatively common reasons as to why a car would suddenly stop in traffic, this allows the AI to then consider that the car might be stopped due to a driver traffic guardian. This is not a certainty that the situation entails a driver traffic guardian. Just as humans can only guess when they experience such a moment, likewise the AI is also going to be "guessing" that the situation involves a traffic guardian.

I mention this aspect about "guessing" since there are some conventional systems developers that are not particularly used to dealing with uncertainties and probabilities in terms of their coding practices. They write programs that they expect will repeatedly and always do whatever they do without any notion of the "chances" of things occurring or not occurring. In AI development, and especially a human endeavor such as driving a car, you have to alter your programming mindset to include the use of uncertainties and probabilities.

Also, in terms of identifying traffic situations that might include the act of a traffic guardian, it is possible via analyzing large-scale datasets of traffic data to be able to more readily spot such moments. Using Machine Learning (ML) and deep learning, usually consisting of Artificial Neural Networks (ANN), you can deeply analyze thousands upon thousands of traffic situations and train the neural network to be able to identify the driver traffic guardian aspects. When a driving situation begins to arise, the ML can potentially participate in making the detection of it.

The context of the detected driving situation will then shape what action the AI self-driving car should next take. It could be that the AI will opt to proceed and make use of the traffic guardian's actions. Or, it could be that the AI will opt to wait it out and not exploit the traffic guardian's actions.

The AI might even opt to take some other action such as had I been able to maneuver in my mall exit predicament, I might have decided to not even exit onto the street at all, and perhaps proceed to drive in the mall parking lot to another exit that allowed for a less chancy way of getting out of the mall. The AI needs to consider this possibility too of escaping the situation altogether.

Here's another twist for you. So far, I've focused on having the AI self-driving car detect and react to a driver traffic guardian. Perhaps what's good for the goose is good for the gander.

In essence, would we want to have the AI be able to act as a driver traffic guardian?

Your first knee-jerk reaction to the question is likely that you would not want the AI to be a traffic guardian. Let it do the simple things of just safely navigating traffic. But, I would argue that if we are desirous of having AI that can drive as a human drivers, clearly there are some situations that being a traffic guardian can be advantageous.

I've not intended herein to suggest that a traffic guardian is always by definition wrong in what they are doing. There are situations in our driving days that involve the useful deployment of being a traffic guardian. It is admittedly not an easy ploy to pull off. There is also the complication that the AI self-driving car doesn't have a ready means to wave and do head gestures, which a human driver can do and thus convey potentially their intention when doing a traffic guardian play.

Nonetheless, we argue that the AI should have a module or capability to be able to instigate a driver traffic guardian action. This needs to be done with great care. It would need to be undertaken sparingly. It would need to be executed well. And, if something begins to go awry, the AI needs to avoid being dogmatic and must be able to adjust, including abandoning the traffic guardian act for the moment at-hand.

There are some AI developers that bemoan the idea of having to craft a capability to be able to contend with driver traffic guardians. They point out that they perceive this matter to be an edge problem. An edge problem is a portion of a larger problem and it is considered at the edge or corner of the mainstay of the problem being solved. We're not so convinced it is an edge problem.

The aspect of the AI self-driving car being able to on its own instigate a driver traffic guardian action does fit more so into the edge problem category.

Generally, we assert that the detection and contending with a traffic guardian should be a core part of the AI's capabilities for driving a self-driving car. The next advancement of having an AI self-driving car that can leverage as a driving tactic the initiation of being a traffic guardian is not quite as essential and therefore could be lumped into the edge problems bucket.

Either way, the traffic guardian elements are vital to driving safely.

Driver traffic guardians, love them or hate them. You likely have faced driving situations wherein a traffic guardian has helped you out and you were heart warmed that someone would care enough to give you an opportunity to make a driving maneuver that you otherwise felt jammed on. There are probably many other occasions wherein a misguided traffic guardian created a bottled-up nightmare and you figured the person was an utter dolt.

Let's make sure that the AI of a self-driving car can contend with traffic guardians, both the appropriate ones and the dolts, and ensure that the self-driving car is able to act in a responsible manner that helps ensure safety for all. That's the kind of automated driving guardians we need on our roads.

CHAPTER 8
ANTI-GRIDLOCK LAWS
AND
AI SELF-DRIVING CARS

CHAPTER 8

ANTI-GRIDLOCK LAWS
AND
AI SELF-DRIVING CARS

I call it the Evil Knievel intersection.

During my morning commute, I drive through a rather troublesome Los Angeles intersection that I affectionately refer to as the Evil Knievel. I've co-opted the name of the famous motorcyclist Evel Knievel that was known for having jumped over numerous cars, buses, live animals, and many other intimidating objects, and well known for his quest to do a motorcycle jump across the Grand Canyon (he instead opted to try jumping across the Snake River Canyon).

In all of his myriad of jump variants, he always began with a takeoff point on one side, a leap-of-faith to make the precarious crossing, and then he'd aim to safely land on a landing ramp on the other side. You likely know that he often was unable to make the jumps unscathed and ended-up incurring more than 400+ broken bones and fractures, placing him into the Guinness Book of World Records as the person that survived the most broken bones in a lifetime.

The reason that I invoke this imagery is that the intersection that I cross each day is one that often is prone to gridlock. When I use the word "gridlock" it is meant to suggest that cars will at times enter into the intersection while the light is green and fail to make it fully across the intersection before the light turns red, ending up stranded in the intersection and serving to block traffic. You've undoubtedly experienced being blocked by cars that were momentarily stranded in an intersection. And if so, you were probably irked (pissed off!) that those drivers misjudged the situation and are blocking your fully legal efforts to get across the intersection.

Here in California, we are known for having been one of the first states to enact an anti-gridlock law that specifically prohibits the blocking of an intersection, doing so in 1987, and it reads as follows:

"A driver of a vehicle shall not enter an intersection or marked crosswalk unless there is sufficient space on the other side of the intersection or marked crosswalk to accommodate the vehicle driven without obstructing the through passage of vehicles from either side." California Vehicle Code Section 22526.

The law itself seems rather self-evident and easy to understand. Well, of course you should not enter into an intersection unless you know that you can make it to the other side. Seems pretty simple. Basic driving 101, as they say.

But, why did the chicken attempt to cross the road? Because it was hoping to get to the other side, and if it couldn't do so it figured that being part-way there was better than not any of the way there at all. I think that's how the old joke goes, though maybe I've augmented it a bit.

Each morning, I see chickens, uh, make that drivers, whom are seeking to get across the intersection. They can plainly see that there is traffic on the other side of the intersection. They can plainly see that the traffic on the other side is completely choked full and backed-up all the way to the crosswalk. There is no chance of squeezing into that morass. And yet, there are drivers that start into the intersection anyway.

Why do they do so?

One form of logic is that the impatient driver hopes that by the time the light goes red, the traffic on the other side will have moved forward, and therefore they will indeed safely and fully make it across the intersection. They are betting that the traffic up ahead will move on a timely basis to allow them to make it across. Often times these hopeful drivers make a lousy bet and it turns out the traffic up ahead stays put. This means that the driver becomes stranded in the intersection and will be blocking traffic that is trying to next move through the intersection from the perpendicular side.

The cars that are blocked by the interloper are likely to get rather riled-up about the situation. Even if you've gotten stuck in the middle of intersection previously, you likely have little sympathy for others that do so. You perhaps were even berated by other drivers when you were in the middle of the intersection, and so you might be inclined to berate other drivers for their similar transgression.

Sometimes the stranded car inspires other drivers to honk their horns at the driver. This used to be a common occurrence in many downtown cities that experience much gridlock. You would hear a continual stream of honking horns due to the continual pattern of cars stuck in the middle of intersections.

In California, we passed a law that says you are only to honk your horn if it will facilitate safe driving. If you opt to use your horn and it is construed by a police officer as not being conducive to safe driving, you can get a ticket for honking your horn.

Is the honking of a horn at a driver that is stranded in the middle of an intersection a form of facilitating safe driving? Likely not. You might try to argue that by honking your horn you are forewarning the stranded driver that they are doing something that is unsafe. I'd expect that a police officer would say that the stranded driver likely already knew that and did not need a honking horn to make them aware of it. You might argue that your horn is aiding other drivers that might not realize the car is stranded in the intersection and thus you are trying to save other drivers. I can imagine the police officer rolling their eyes at that one.

Each morning I see car after car that ends-up in the middle of the intersection and awaits a hopeful chance of making it to the other side. You can see the look in their eyes as they anxiously try to watch the traffic signal and pretend that it will forever remain green, and simultaneously they are looking at the traffic up ahead and praying that it will move forward. Enough cars succeed that it does not always lead to a blocked intersection. The horn honking is relatively minimal, though the frustration level of the other drivers can get pretty high.

There are some drivers that will butt up against the tail-end of the traffic that is on the other side of the intersection. They often are completely covering the crosswalk. They are also likely somewhat protruding into the intersection via the rear portion of their car. This seems like a better spot to be than to be utterly in the middle of the intersection.

What happens next is a dance of the partially gridlocked intersection.

Pedestrians using the crosswalk will try to walk either behind the stranded car or go in front of the stranded car.

For those pedestrians that opt to go in front of the stranded car, they are essentially blocking the car from being able to move forward if perchance the traffic moves during the time that those pedestrians are crossing the crosswalk. The driver will get frustrated at those pedestrians because the driver wants to extricate themselves from their stranded position and now the pesky pedestrians are in the way.

I've seen some drivers that inch forward to try and suggest to the pedestrians that they should stop blocking the stranded car and allow the car to move forward. The logic too is that if the stranded car can move forward sufficiently to no longer block the crosswalk, it will make life easier for the pedestrians that are trying to use the crosswalk. Unfortunately, it's all a knotted-up situation and the pedestrians are so eager to get through the crosswalk that they don't really care whether the car is able to move forward or not. To them, the car is in the way and they are going to go around it, either in front or from the rear of the car.

For those pedestrians that try to walk behind the stranded car, they are now dangerously verging into the intersection. They are no longer in the crosswalk and instead are walking around the posterior of the car and therefore stepping directly into the intersection. This can be dicey because there are likely cars now going through the intersection and those cars can be getting quite close to the posterior of the protruding car. A pedestrian can get squeezed between the proverbial rock and a hard place, namely be positioned between the rear-end of the stranded car and a moving car that is within perhaps inches of that protruding car.

From the perspective of the cars that are trying to get through the intersection, and for which there is now a car sitting in the crosswalk and protruding into the intersection, you've got a kind of dance that arises there. The cars that are closest to the stranded car will need to judge whether they can make it safely past the posterior and remain in the lane of traffic. At times, those cars will not be able to make it in their own lane and thus need to decide whether to come to a stop, or whether to try and swing into the lane next to them.

If the driver opts to swing into the lane next to them, this can cause the drivers in that lane to then be confounded. Some of those cars might be moving very fast and figure that the blockage of the protruding car doesn't directly impact them and so they are just going to zoom through the intersection. Meanwhile, the cars in the lane that is partially blocked are fishing around and trying to see how much they can swerve into that other lane without actually causing a crash.

As perhaps is evident, the driver that is in the crosswalk has done a lot to make the entire intersection an unsafe place. The pedestrians that are walking in front of the stranded car are at risk, and could get hit by that anxious driver trying to move forward. The pedestrians walking behind the stranded car are at risk, since a car that is trying to cross the intersection might hit them or hit the rear of the protruding car. The cars in the lane closest to the protruding car and having to veer dangerous around it and possibly disrupting other traffic that is now trying to cross the intersection.

It is a dangerously cascading and unsafe situation, all because of that driver that thought they could try to squeeze into the other side of the intersection but misjudged the matter.

There is the other variant of a car that gets stranded fully in the intersection and cannot make it to even the edge of the other side. In that case, other cars that now have a green light will try to flow around the stranded car. It is like having a big rock placed into the middle of a stream. The water tries to flow around the rock, either behind the rock or in front of the rock. Likewise, cars try to go to the right or left of the stranded car.

This is another highly dangerous situation. Any of those cars could hit the stranded car. Any of those cars could hit each other. A driver coming up upon the intersection might not be watching for a car that is stranded in the intersection and plow right into it. Traffic is also being slowed down by the stranded car and it will likely reduce the number of cars that can successfully get through the intersection in the green light allowed.

The driver in the stranded car might also try to move ahead, in spite of the cars flowing around it. Imagine s rock in a stream wherein the rock decides to move. This can be confusing to the other drivers.

The stranded car driver figures that if they can even crawl forward and possibly make it to the edge of the intersection, it is better than being in the middle of the intersection. But this crawling action can make matters much worse. The other cars are not able to readily predict where the stranded but now moving car is going to be. In some cases, it is almost better to just sit still and hope for the best, rather than trying to clear the intersection but then getting plowed by other cars that have no idea where you are going (though yes, I realize in theory it is best to be completely clear of the intersection, I am just saying that at the moment in time of choosing whether to move ahead or not, it is not so easy a choice).

So far, I've focused on just one car that might get stranded either in the intersection or at the edge of an intersection. There could be more than one car that gets into such a pickle. If you have a multitude of cars that all decide to try and get through the intersection and are unsuccessful, it is as though a dam have been built by an eager beaver in that intersection. The dam will hold-back traffic that is now wanting to use the intersection and legally has a green light to do so.

That's when you get true gridlock.

The basis for calling it gridlock is that most downtown areas are structured into a series of streets that resemble a grid. In your mind, think of a spreadsheet with rows and columns. You've got streets that intersect with each other on this grid. New York City is probably the most notable grid structured downtown area.

The grid of streets can get boxed-up by the fundamental aspect of blocking an intersection. If you block one intersection, it can cause the traffic coming into that intersection to get stopped. This can cascade to other intersections. If everyone opts to flood into the intersections and block them too, you effectively lock-up the entire grid and no one can move.

Before the advent of anti-gridlock laws, the gridlock situation would often go wildly out-of-control. It might start rather small, such as one intersection gets blocked, but the effect would spread like a rampant virus and quickly the entire grid would get overwhelmed. It is a nightmare to be stuck in it.

There is also no easy solution to undo the swamped grid once it has gotten into a gridlocked mode. It is almost like having twine that is so interwound that you cannot figure out how to untie it. If you move this string of the twine, it might make things worse. When dealing with humans driving their cars, you also cannot expect they will necessarily be overly helpful in undoing a gridlock.

In fact, the traffic gridlock situation is a fascinating indicator of human behavior. If all the human drivers were completely cooperative, the mutual cooperation of politely keeping the intersection free would mean that the traffic would flow nicely. Mutual cooperation in this case begets mutual benefit. The trouble though is that we humans are endowed with a sense of "greed" and therefore what might be good overall is not necessarily as good for you in particular. You are seeking to maximize your own benefits, which might or might not coincide with maximizing it for everyone all-told.

If you abide by leaving the intersection open, let's say it means that it will take you an added 5 minutes to get to work. On the other hand, if you try to buck the system and rush the intersection, even if you get stuck in it, perhaps you are able to avoid those added 5 minutes and get to work sooner. If you do get stuck, you run the risk of a car accident, but you are so focused on the timing of making progress that you aren't clearly thinking about the risks per se.

There are some morning drivers that I've observed routinely are seemingly happy to block the intersection. They appear to believe that other drivers will be more civil than them, and thus the risks of getting hit by another car is slim, or so they believe. The scofflaws also don't seem to care about the California law that clearly says they are wrong to do what they are doing.

One reason that these lawbreakers might not care about the long-arm of the law is that it is a difficult law to enforce.

Think about it. Let's assume that a police officer has to be present to witness the act of your blocking the intersection. What are the odds of a police officer happening to be there when you make your untoward move? Probably low odds that a police officer will be nearby (and, if you are being intentional and devious, presumably you were on the look for the cops and if you didn't see a police officer you then took your chance at blocking the intersection).

If a police officer happens to be present and sees you blocking the intersection, they need to presumably try to pull you over to chat with you and likely issue you a ticket. The act of pulling you over is certainly going to disrupt traffic even more so than the stranded car does. Also, if there are a multitude of cars in the intersection, which of them will the officer try to stop? You figure that it hopefully won't be you and the officer will pick some other scofflaw instead.

Here, the ticket is only considered a parking ticket, unless the intersection has a posted warning sign or unless you perform some other kind of untoward act, and in that case it is a moving violation ticket. Thus, you are likely hoping that if you do actually get caught, the officer will only issue you a parking ticket. A parking ticket is easy to deal with and you won't usually get any dinged points on your driving record.

In general, and especially for a bold scofflaw, they will likely decide it is "better" to try and get stuck in the middle of the intersection or make it to an edge, presumably allowing them to reduce their travel time and get to their destination sooner, for them alone, and that since the likelihood of getting caught seems relatively low, and even if they do get caught the nature of the penalty will likely be low, it all adds up to a go-for-it mentality.

Some locales have mounted intersection cameras to catch these scofflaws. This helps to deal with the aspect of not readily having a police officer around to see the act and also it reduces the time and disruption to traffic of an officer issuing a ticket. On the downside, the cost of setting up the cameras and its actual role in being able to discourage the scofflaws all tends to make it not particularly viable as a solution to preventing the gridlock instigators (they also have at times tried to fight the law, when caught, by claiming issues associated with the cameras).

It is actually kind of surprising that I don't see more cars stranded in the middle of the Evil Knievel intersection each morning. I'd guess that it is partially due to a cultural aspect. Those that have calculated the odds of getting caught will tend to realize pretty quickly that it is not so much the law that will get them as it is their fellow drivers on the roadways. When cars do get stranded, the anger from the other drivers is quite palatable. I've not seen actual efforts to dismount from cars and go to fisticuffs, but the sense overall seems to be that those intruding on others by blocking intersections are somehow going to get bad karma (Ha, that's a California thing, for sure!).

In quick recap, you can have partial gridlock or you can full-on gridlock. There are some drivers that know exactly what they are doing and don't care that they might get stuck in the intersection. There are other drivers that misjudge the situation and are hoping they will make it to the other side. There are some that figure it is sufficient if they make it to the other side and block the crosswalk. All in all, most of these drivers are not particularly giving much weight to the dangers they are creating and the unsafe nature of their efforts. They've either decided the odds of getting hurt are low or they are oblivious to the chances of creating a collision and causing injury or death.

What does this have to do with AI self-driving cars?

At the Cybernetic AI Self-Driving Car Institute, we are developing AI software for self-driving cars. One core aspect involves the AI being able to contend with the potential of gridlock situations.

Allow me to elaborate.

I'd like to first clarify and introduce the notion that there are varying levels of AI self-driving cars. The topmost level is considered Level 5. A Level 5 self-driving car is one that is being driven by the AI and there is no human driver involved. For the design of Level 5 self-driving cars, the auto makers are even removing the gas pedal, brake pedal, and steering wheel, since those are contraptions used by human drivers. The Level 5 self-driving car is not being driven by a human and nor is there an expectation that a human driver will be present in the self-driving car. It's all on the shoulders of the AI to drive the car.

For self-driving cars less than a Level 5, there must be a human driver present in the car. The human driver is currently considered the responsible party for the acts of the car. The AI and the human driver are co-sharing the driving task. In spite of this co-sharing, the human is supposed to remain fully immersed into the driving task and be ready at all times to perform the driving task. I've repeatedly warned about the dangers of this co-sharing arrangement and predicted it will produce many untoward results.

Let's focus herein on the true Level 5 self-driving car. Much of the comments apply to the less than Level 5 self-driving cars too, but the fully autonomous AI self-driving car will receive the most attention in this discussion.

Here's the usual steps involved in the AI driving task:

- Sensor data collection and interpretation

- Sensor fusion

- Virtual world model updating

- AI action planning

- Car controls command issuance

Another key aspect of AI self-driving cars is that they will be driving on our roadways in the midst of human driven cars too. There are some pundits of AI self-driving cars that continually refer to a utopian world in which there are only AI self-driving cars on the public roads. Currently there are about 250+ million conventional cars in the United States alone, and those cars are not going to magically disappear or become true Level 5 AI self-driving cars overnight.

Indeed, the use of human driven cars will last for many years, likely many decades, and the advent of AI self-driving cars will occur while there are still human driven cars on the roads. This is a crucial point since this means that the AI of self-driving cars needs to be able to contend with not just other AI self-driving cars, but also contend with human driven cars.

It is easy to envision a simplistic and rather unrealistic world in which all AI self-driving cars are politely interacting with each other and being civil about roadway interactions. That's not what is going to be happening for the foreseeable future. AI self-driving cars and human driven cars will need to be able to cope with each other.

Returning to the topic of gridlocks, here's what we need to consider for the AI of an AI self-driving car:

- Detect that a gridlock exists when it is there,

- Determine how to best maneuver within a partially gridlocked intersection,

- Deal with stranded cars that are sitting in a crosswalk,

- Be on the watch for cars behind you that might get panicked due to a brewing gridlock,

- Avoid getting stuck in the middle of an intersection as part of a gridlock,

- Don't instigate the starting of a gridlock,

- Aid other cars as to dealing with the gridlock if feasible to do so

- Other

There are some AI developers that would assert that there is nothing special for the AI to do about a gridlock situation. For them, the normal everyday operation of the self-driving car should be sufficient for dealing with gridlocks. If the AI can drive a self-driving car and navigate the roadways, it is perceived by the AI developers that there is nothing extraordinary about the gridlock circumstances and therefore no special attention is needed.

We disagree.

The gridlock circumstance is a special case and requires a specialized module or capability to be handled.

It might well be considered an "edge" problem by some, namely that it is not necessarily at the core of what the AI needs to do to drive a car minimally. There are though so many driving aspects that are entangled with the capability of dealing with gridlocks that we argue it is not readily classified as an edge problem and needs to be placed higher up in the priority of aspects needing to be dealt with by the AI.

Some AI developers use the piped piper approach of having the AI simply follow a car that is ahead of the self-driving car. This is not a wise move necessarily for the gridlock situation. Just because the car ahead of you opts to go into the intersection does not mean you should too.

You've likely seen many times that cars sit at the intersection waiting to rush across it, the moment that there is a spot open on the other side. Typically, one car at a time opts to make a dash across the intersection. It is as though a door opens momentarily on the other side and so one car can make it into that door. The door then closes for a moment. If the door opens again, another car makes the dash.

If you blindly follow a car that is making the dash to the other side, you are likely going to end-up starting the gridlock because the other car will make it but you won't. That's why many times you'll see a gridlock start to form. One or more cars tried to follow one lead car, and the lead car made it across while the other cars did not. Those other cars are now stranded and panicked.

So, the pied piper approach won't cut it. The AI needs to be looking further ahead and trying to predict whether or not there is a viable opening for the AI self-driving car to make it fully across the intersection.

I am sure there are some AI developers will say that the problem is the human driver. If we had only AI self-driving cars, they would all be civil toward each other and not cause any blocking of any intersections. Furthermore, they could use their V2V (vehicle-to-vehicle) electronic communications to ensure they coordinated their efforts. If somehow an AI self-driving car did get stranded in an intersection, it would merely use V2V to forewarn all other nearby self-driving cars.

As I mentioned earlier, we are not going to have the Utopian world of only AI self-driving cars, certainly not for a very long time from now. Thus, cross out the "there won't ever be gridlock" notion for the foreseeable future.

In terms of identifying traffic situations that might include the emergence of a gridlock, it is possible via analyzing large-scale datasets of traffic data to be able to more readily spot such moments. Using Machine Learning (ML) and deep learning, usually consisting of Artificial Neural Networks (ANN), you can deeply analyze thousands upon thousands of traffic situations and train the neural network to be able to identify the potential gridlock aspects. When a driving situation begins to arise, the ML can potentially participate in making the detection of it.

The context of the detected driving situation will then shape what action the AI self-driving car should next take.

It could be that the AI will opt to proceed cautiously and not get stuck in the middle of the intersection. Or, it could be that the AI will opt to wait it out and try to step into the matter after some iterations of the traffic signal, hopefully without further exasperating the gridlock.

The AI needs to consider the possibility too of escaping the situation altogether – I've done the same when some mornings I take a different route to work that avoids the Evel Knievel intersection, or I stay in the rightmost lane and if the intersection is especially testy that day I then opt to make a right turn and forego trying to get across that particular intersection.

I realize that some AI developers try to reduce the complexity of the situation to a simpleton perspective. They would say that if the AI self-driving car comes up to an intersection and the light is green, all the AI needs to do is calculate the time remaining on the green light and the distance and time needed to reach the other intersection. If the numbers don't look good, then the AI self-driving car should just sit still and not try to make the leap across the intersection.

It's not that easy.

For example, I've sat at the front of the Evel Knievel intersection and watched carefully the advent of the green light, along with knowing how long the green light lasts, I know the amount of time it takes for me to scoot across the intersection. I'd wager that most people don't know how long a green light will last and so only have a hunch about it, and nor do they know how long it takes to drive across an intersection. The average driver just does this by gut feel. In my case, I've driven this intersection so many times that I know exactly how long the green light will last and how long it takes for me to drive across the intersection.

You also need to consider that you cannot just gun it and zip across the intersection at 80 miles per hour. There is the need to come to a reasonable stop when you've reached the other side. You need to be able to maintain control of your car while in the intersection. You need to be watching in case any pedestrians suddenly decide to cross, even if jaywalking. There are a lot of added factors about making the scoot across the intersection.

Furthermore, you need to include the factor of the other cars nearby to you and what actions they might take.

Here's one of my "favorite" actions that often catches other drivers completely off-guard. Suppose you are sitting at the front of the intersection and trying to decide whether to proceed. Meanwhile, in the lane next to you, a car has proceeded forward, but they timed it poorly and are now stranded in the intersection and are sticking out like a sore thumb.

For your lane, let's suppose that your lane as it exists on the other side of the intersection suddenly gets an opening to allow a car to fit into the lane.

You could in theory scoot over and take that position, doing so because you are "guaranteed" that there is a spot open. But, the other car, the one stranded in the intersection, and yet in a different lane, realizes they could snatch your open spot, and so they switch lanes mid-intersection and move into your spot.

If you had already started into the intersection, you now are the loner that sticks out like a sore thumb.

At the moment you began into the intersection, you had an opening on the other side. The other driver though as taken it from you, doing so in a manner that caught you unawares. If you were merely calculating the distance and the time, you would have most certainly calculated that you could make it to the other side safely. A simplistic mathematical formula is insufficient, I assure you.

Generally, we assert that the detection and contending with gridlocks should be a core part of the AI's capabilities for driving a self-driving car. It involves sophisticated driving tactics and cannot be ignored, nor can it be handled by formulaic expressions.

Gridlock detection and maneuvering are vital to an AI self-driving car being able to drive safely in real-world driving situations.

Traffic gridlocks.

We all abhor them.

Yet, our very own actions can spur them. Even if your locale does not have laws that specifically ban gridlocks, it is likely that if gridlock begins to grow, there will be a backlash against those drivers that spark them.

An AI self-driving car needs to be an active participant in aiding anti-gridlock actions. Just like the old question about chickens, we need to ask, why did the AI self-driving car try to cross the road? The answer ought to be because it ascertained that it was safe to do so and accomplished the feat like a champ.

.

CHAPTER 9
ARGUING MACHINES
AND
AI SELF-DRIVING CARS

Lance B. Eliot

CHAPTER 9

ARGUING MACHINES

AND

AI SELF-DRIVING CARS

I'd like to argue with you. Ready?

No, I don't think you are ready. What's that, you say that you are ready. I don't think so. You insist that you are ready to argue? Sorry, it doesn't seem like you are ready.

If you've ever seen the now-classic Monty Python skit about arguments, my aforementioned attempt to argue with you might seem familiar. In the skit, a man goes to an argument "clinic" that allows you to pay money to argue with a professional arguer. At one point, the man seeking an argument gets upset that the arguer is merely acting in a contradictory way and not truly providing an argument. They then argue about whether contradiction itself is a valid form of arguing, which the man paying for the argument insists is a hollow form of arguing and not intellectually in the spirit of a true argument.

It is a rather clever and memorable skit.

I bring up the notion of arguing and arguments due to the emerging approach of using "arguing machines" in the realm of AI. I'd like to share with you various facets of the arguing machines approach and also establish how it relates to AI self-driving cars.

Take a look at Figure 1.

Eliot Framework: AI Arguing Machines

Figure 1

Maturity Matrix

Criteria of Arguing Machines Approach	Level C: Initial	Level B: Capable	Level C: Master
Outcome Indication	AI Instance Status	Proposed Result or Action	Proposed Result or Action
Argument Structure Presented	No	No	Yes
Chooser/Arbitrator Capability	Simple	Moderate	Advanced
Human Supervisor	Yes	Yes	No
Disagreement Declaration	Based on Status (Binary Indicator)	Based on Difference (Single Attribute)	Based on Differences (Multi-Attribute)
Judicial Automated Acumen	None	Minimal	Expansive
AI Primary/Secondary Instances (1:N)	Glass Box	Black Box	Black Box

Copyright © 2018, Dr. Lance B. Eliot. AI Cybernetic Self-Driving Car Institute.

I've depicted a maturity matrix framework for AI Arguing Machines, which I'll be covering herein.

The matrix encompasses some of the key criteria or characteristics that distinguish between various AI Arguing Machines approaches.

The maturity levels range from lowest (Level C) to highest (Level A).

The lowest level is considered an Initial approach (Level C), the next level is labeled as Capable (Level B), and the highest or most extensive approach is referred to as the Master level (Level A).

With fail-safe AI systems the intent is to craft AI systems that are somewhat fail-safe (i.e., safe to fail), and thus you often will have a primary AI system and a secondary AI system.

The primary AI system is let's say assigned to be the key runner of whatever is taking place, while the secondary AI system is typically there as a back-up in case the primary AI somehow fails or suspects that it is failing.

You might setup the primary AI to do a kind of self-diagnosis and if it begins to believe that it is having internal troubles, it might handover the AI tasks at-hand to the secondary AI. There could be an ongoing handshake taking place between the primary AI and the secondary AI, and at some point the primary AI can turn over the effort to the secondary AI, or, if the primary AI does not on a timely basis perform the handshake you could have the secondary AI assume that the primary AI is in trouble and thus forcibly take over the task from the primary AI.

There are a variety of means to setup the relationship and nature of which should be running, whether the primary AI should be, or the secondary AI should be.

You can use a "Chooser" that will try to decide which of the AI instances should be used.

We might have more than just a primary AI and a secondary AI, in that we might have some N number of AI instances, all of which are able to perform the same tasks, and all of which can be potentially chosen to run the task at-hand. We'll refer to the primary AI as the instance 1, and the secondary as instance 2, and so on, all of which are actively executing and keeping up with the tasks underway. Thus, the Chooser can select from any of them, under the belief that they are all ready and active to step into the role of being the actual "primary" AI undertaking the task at-hand.

Typically, there is a "switching cost" involved in turning over execution to another of the active instances, therefore the Chooser needs to be cautious of opting to arbitrarily just turn over the task to any of the other available and viable AI instances. To switch over to another AI instance might introduce latency and if the AI is performing a real-time task, the matter of time is crucial to whatever chore is being performed.

By-and-large, the Chooser will be tending toward allowing an AI instance to become the primary and stick with it, until or if there is a circumstance that suggests the AI instance is no longer able to properly undertake the chores.

Thrashing about by continually switching from one AI instance to another would be likely problematic. Plus, presumably once the Chooser has switched away from an AI instance, it is likely due to a failure of the AI instance, and resuming that AI instance might be dicey since it might no longer be adequately able to perform the tasks at-hand.

The Chooser aka Arbitrator or Judge

How might the Chooser decide which of the available and active AI instances is a suitable choice?

A simplistic method involves having an AI instance provide a status indicator and as long as the status indicator seems to be positive or good, the Chooser can select that AI instance. Thus, we might begin the task with AI instance 1 (known as the primary AI at that juncture), and the Chooser is keeping tabs on the status indicators of the AI instances of 1 to N. If the current primary AI indicates a "bad" status indication, the Chooser could then select any of the remaining AI instances that are still reporting a positive or "good" indication.

The selection might not be done in a random manner, and instead it could be that the AI instances have been lined-up in a sequence that is preferred for selection. In that case, the AI instance 1, when no longer seemingly good, the Chooser would switch over the tasks to AI instance 2. AI instance 2 then becomes the "primary" AI for the moment. If it goes to a "bad" indicator status, the Chooser would switch things over to AI instance 3. And so on.

Rather than having each of the AI instances report a status indicator, another approach would be to have each instance present what it is intending to do next.

For example, suppose the task involves steering an AI self-driving car. The current primary AI might indicate that the next act of steering is to involve having the steering wheel angle turn to degree X. Meanwhile, the secondary AI might indicate that the steering wheel angle should be the degree Y. We'll use just the two AI instances in this example for now, though as I've mentioned there could be N number of them.

The Chooser could inspect the primary AI's indication of X and compare it to the secondary AI's indication of Y. If the X and Y are approximately equal, the Chooser might consider this as a sign of agreement between the primary AI and the secondary AI. Since there is agreement, the Chooser has no need to switch from the primary AI and allows the primary AI to proceed.

Notice that I mentioned that the X and Y are considered "in agreement" if they are approximately equal. I say this because the primary AI and the secondary AI might have different methods of ascertaining the steering wheel angles and thus, they might differ somewhat about the particular amount. If the difference is considered miniscule and not substantive, it is not worth the effort to declare a disagreement. The amount of variance allowed between the two would be dependent upon the nature of the element being used and the Chooser would need to have some pre-defined basis for declaring that a difference was substantive.

Let's suppose that the X and Y are indeed substantively different, and the Chooser now needs to decide whether to continue with the primary AI that provided the X or to switch over to using the secondary AI that provided the Y.

We have returned to the question about how the Chooser is to make a choice between the AI instances. When we had the simplistic approach of a status indicator, it was easy for the Chooser because all it had to do was monitor the status indicators and the moment that the active AI went to a "bad" indicative status it meant that the Chooser should switch over the task to another AI instance.

With this X and Y matter of having a substantive difference between X and Y, should the Chooser assume that the secondary AI is the "right one" and the primary AI is the "wrong one" (meaning that the correct angle to be used is Y and not X). But, it could be that the secondary AI is the "wrong one" and the primary AI is the "right one." Of course, we could decide beforehand that any time that a substantive difference arises, whichever AI is primary must be mistaken and therefore switch over to another instance, though this logic would usually seem suspect.

We could require that the Chooser be more sophisticated and be able to weigh-in about which of the X or Y is the better choice. If the Chooser then ascertained that the X is the better choice, it would presumably continue with the running of the primary AI, while if the Y is the better choice then the Chooser would presumably switch over to the secondary AI.

You might think of this Chooser as a kind of judge in a court of law. There are two parties in the courtroom, the primary AI and the secondary AI. They are standing before the court. One professes that the X is the proper choice. The other professes that Y is the proper choice. The judge is able to determine that X and Y are substantively different. Should the judge opt to say that the primary AI is right and should proceed, or should the judge opt to say that the secondary AI is right and it should proceed instead of the primary AI?

If the judge happens to know a lot about the nature of the task and the meaning of the X and Y, it could be that the judge is sophisticated enough to be able to make the choice without any other input, other than the X and Y that is being presented.

The rub is that the more sophisticated the Chooser becomes (the judge), the more chances of it substituting its judgement in lieu of the presumed more elaborated capabilities of the primary AI and the secondary AI. In that sense, we're almost then placing the Chooser into the role of being another AI instance that has to be equivalent to the other AI instances involved in performing the task at-hand, but is that what we intend to have happen?

Instead, we might allow for an argument to occur between the primary AI and the secondary AI, of which by presenting the argument to the Chooser, it can base a selection of either the primary AI or the secondary AI based on the greater of the prevailing arguments. We could then refer to the Chooser as a judge or an arbitrator. Rather than making a choice based on a simplistic status indicator, and rather than making a somewhat random choice if the X and Y produced are substantively different, we might have the Chooser act as a judge or arbitrator that entertains respective arguments from each party and uses those arguments as part of the criteria for making a switching decision.

In short, here's our rules:

- If the primary AI and the secondary AI are in agreement about the next action, which could be ascertained by comparing their next action choices of X and Y respectively and allowing that they are in agreement if the difference is considered negligible with respect to whatever has been predefined as a non-substantive difference, the Chooser (aka judge or arbitrator) allows the primary AI to continue ahead.

- If the primary AI and the secondary AI are in disagreement about the next action, which was ascertained by the detection of a substantive difference in their next action choices of X and Y respectively, the Chooser (aka judge or arbitrator) requests and inspects arguments from the primary AI and the secondary AI to then make a choice as to whether to continue ahead with the primary AI or to switch to the secondary AI.

- These above rules can be recast in the matter of having some N instances of the AI system and thus is not limited to just having two AI systems in-hand.

Assuming that the AI system is an integral part of a real-time system, and for which the real-time system involves life-and-death matters such as those involved in the driving task of an AI self-driving car, the Chooser must be streamlined to handle the assessment of the arguments, and too the AI instances must be able to rapidly present their arguments.

Timing Crucial to Making Choices

I mention this timing aspect because we are adding overhead to the whole mechanism of what is taking place for choosing the next action. Any delay in executing the next action could have dire consequences. We would need to figure out the appropriate timing allowed for sufficient time to make the final judgment or choice.

A fail-safe on the fail-safe AI might be to have a choice made on some predefined basis that if time runs out while trying to make a choice, any of the available choices is considered "better" than making no choice at all (it's like a chess match in which the timer runs out for you to make a choice, and you are torn about which move to make, but you forfeit the match if you don't make a move, so you then select whatever move seems viable and hope for the best). Or, some other more informed choice mechanism might be employed.

Let's consider the timing aspects. The primary AI needs to figure out and present its argument. The secondary AI needs to figure out and present its argument. The Chooser needs to wait for and then assess the two respective arguments. Once the Chooser has made its choice, we are then at the point of dealing with the switchover costs, as alluded to earlier, assuming that the Chooser opts to switch AI instances after conducting the assessment and making a judgement.

I realize on the surface that the overhead of preparing and presenting arguments would seem at first glance as not viable and actually somewhat crazy to consider. Do keep in mind though that it would be a canned kind of affair. It would be highly questionable if the AI systems were not well prepared to undertake this set of steps about trying to prove or verify their choices. Instead, the AI system and each of the instances is purposely wired-up to perform this task and thus the AI developers would beforehand have tuned it to try and ensure it runs in speedy time.

I used the analogy of a judge in a courtroom. I don't want you to overinflate that analogy. We are used to seeing courtroom dramas that involve quite elaborate arguments and the judge has to keep the parties focused on the case. The AI mechanism for the arguing machines is not going to allow for proclaimed objections by the parties and nor any kind of back-and-forth to try and sway the case. I suppose you might think of this as a cut-and-dried kind of courtroom case, maybe like a streamlined and tightly run Small Claims court. You walk into court, tersely present your case, the judge slams down the gavel and makes a quick choice. On to the next case!

That deals with the timing aspects.

Suppose though that the judge doesn't show-up for the case? This would be equivalent to having the Chooser itself become at fault and perhaps be unable to participate in the arguing machines debate.

In fact, it is dicey that we are setting up a system involving a Single Point of Failure (SPOF), namely that if the Chooser or judge or arbitrator of the AI systems is unable to perform (and we only have one of them), we then have an untoward situation. We might get more elaborate and have multiple Choosers. Or, we might decide that the primary AI will continue unabated and only if it decides to switch over would then the secondary AI take the reins, in the scenario of a Chooser that is absent from the game. And so on.

I'll also mention that if the Chooser or judge or arbitrator shows-up but goes nutty, we still have a problem on our hands and indeed the situation becomes somewhat more troubling than if not being present at all. How will the AI systems be able to realize that the Chooser has gone wild? Again, there would need to be a further fail-safe devised for this scenario.

Impacts for AI Self-Driving Cars

What does this have to do with AI self-driving cars?

At the Cybernetic AI Self-Driving Car Institute, we are developing AI software for self-driving cars. One emerging approach that some AI developers are pursing involves incorporating the use of AI arguing machines into their systems, and for which this is pertinent to AI self-driving car systems too.

Allow me to elaborate.

I'd like to first clarify and introduce the notion that there are varying levels of AI self-driving cars. The topmost level is considered Level 5. A Level 5 self-driving car is one that is being driven by the AI and there is no human driver involved. For the design of Level 5 self-driving cars, the auto makers are even removing the gas pedal, brake pedal, and steering wheel, since those are contraptions used by human drivers. The Level 5 self-driving car is not being driven by a human and nor is there an expectation that a human driver will be present in the self-driving car. It's all on the shoulders of the AI to drive the car.

For self-driving cars less than a Level 5, there must be a human driver present in the car. The human driver is currently considered the responsible party for the acts of the car. The AI and the human driver are co-sharing the driving task. In spite of this co-sharing, the human is supposed to remain fully immersed into the driving task and be ready at all times to perform the driving task. I've repeatedly warned about the dangers of this co-sharing arrangement and predicted it will produce many untoward results.

Let's focus herein on the true Level 5 self-driving car. Much of the comments apply to the less than Level 5 self-driving cars too, but the fully autonomous AI self-driving car will receive the most attention in this discussion.

Here's the usual steps involved in the AI driving task:

- Sensor data collection and interpretation

- Sensor fusion

- Virtual world model updating

- AI action planning

- Car controls command issuance

Another key aspect of AI self-driving cars is that they will be driving on our roadways in the midst of human driven cars too. There are some pundits of AI self-driving cars that continually refer to a utopian world in which there are only AI self-driving cars on the public roads. Currently there are about 250+ million conventional cars in the United States alone, and those cars are not going to magically disappear or become true Level 5 AI self-driving cars overnight.

Indeed, the use of human driven cars will last for many years, likely many decades, and the advent of AI self-driving cars will occur while there are still human driven cars on the roads. This is a crucial point since this means that the AI of self-driving cars needs to be able to contend with not just other AI self-driving cars, but also contend with human driven cars. It is easy to envision a simplistic and rather unrealistic world in which all AI self-driving cars are politely interacting with each other and being civil about roadway interactions. That's not what is going to be happening for the foreseeable future. AI self-driving cars and human driven cars will need to be able to cope with each other.

Returning to the topic of AI arguing machines, I'd like to discuss a recent study done by MIT on the matter and that showcases various facets of this emerging approach.

The MIT study entitled "Arguing Machines: Human Supervision of Black Box AI Systems That Make Life-Critical Decisions" (co-authored by Lex Fridman, Li Ding, Benedikt Jenik, Bryan Reimer, https://hcai.mit.edu/arguing-machines/), provides a quite interesting study of the use of arguing machines. Two use cases are considered, one involving an image classification problem, and the other involving a self-driving car matter.

MIT Study on Arguing Machines

Similar to my earlier herein remarks about arguing machines, the MIT study posits that a crucial challenge for making life-critical system-based decisions encompasses those moments when there is a small margin of allowable error in real-world applications entailing human lives. They use a system arbitrator to ascertain whether there is agreement or disagreement between a primary AI and a secondary AI.

They opted to use an image classification use case due to the aspect that image classification is one of the most studied problems in AI, and if their arguing machines approach could aid or enhance image classification, it would well suggest that the technique can be advantageous to a wide array of AI areas. In essence, if you can improve something that has already had everything but the kitchen sink thrown at it, the odds are that you've got a techniques or approach that could help in many other circumstances, including ones that are not nearly as well solved or studied.

For the image classification experiment, they used the popular ResNet image classifier as the primary AI and the also equally popular VGG as the secondary AI. Images were chosen from the ImageNet Dataset.

Note that they two AI systems are entirely different from each other and are not somehow clones or near duplicates. I mention this aspect because there are some that at times assume that the primary AI and the secondary AI would be near copies of one another, but this is not necessarily the case. They can each be devised to try and solve the same problem, likely meeting the same or equivalent set of requirements, and yet make use of completely different algorithms and methods at arriving at their efforts.

The AI instances involved in a fail-safe AI operation can each be designed and developed by separate teams. The instances could have been developed at different times. They might differ in the programming languages used and the AI techniques included. What is key would be that the AI instances are performing the same set of tasks and therefore each in their own "black box" way is trying to accomplish the same tasks at-hand. If that were not the case and they were doing varying tasks, it would no longer be the case that they would be considered straight-ahead failovers for each other.

One particularly fascinating aspect about the experiment was that the both ResNet and VGG make use of deep convolutional neural networks, and both had been trained on the same dataset, and yet they did not "fail" in the same manner during the experimental testing. In other words, you might at first assume that they would both agree almost entirely, and even if they were wrong, they would both be wrong at the same time. This was not the case. As the researchers pointed out, the result suggests and provides further impetus to have other means to gauge the outcomes of AI systems, such as the use of arguing machines.

Furthermore, the arguing machines approach they utilized was able to do an admirable job in terms of improving the image classification performance. This highlights that the act of having two AI systems and monitoring their disagreements can be a significant booster towards reducing errors and aiding performance.

In the second use case, the researchers used again an argument arbitrator, which they referred to also as a disagreement function, and focused on the automated lane-keeping feature of the Tesla Autopilot. Included in their experiment was a dataset of 6,500 disengagements, which are circumstances wherein a human back-up operator opted to disengage the Autopilot. They developed a 5-layered convolutional neural network which would serve as the secondary AI. The primary AI was the Tesla Autopilot software. The researches also devised two key metrics, a False Accept Rate (FAR) and a False Reject Rate (FRR), enabling them to compare the performance of the disagreement system.

Impressively, they further explored the approach by constructing a real-time version that ran while inside an in-motion Tesla car. They used a NVIDIA Jeston TX2 for running of the model, developed and installed a custom interface to connect with the CAN bus of the car, put in place a dashboard-mounted Logitech C920 camera, and used OpenCV for the live video streaming aspects. The devised neural network made use of PyTorch.

I had earlier mentioned the importance of figuring out the timing aspects, and in this case they were able to get the latency down to 200 milliseconds or less, counting from the time of the camera input to the point of a screen GUI update display with the result.

The output factor consisted of the steering angle.

The researchers indicated they used this setup even in evening rush hour traffic, which assuming this took place in Boston, I'd rate their evening rush hour as snarled and messed-up as the traffic here in Los Angeles (therefore presenting a rather invigorating challenge!).

The MIT study is a great example of the potential for AI arguing machines and provides a handy launching pad from which future work can build upon.

Expansion of the AI Arguing Machines Framework

One aspect about the study was that it included the use of a human supervisor as integral to the experimental setup. The machine-based arbitrator consults with a human supervisor. This squarely puts the human-in-the-loop. For AI self-driving cars less than Level 5, this showcases that there is an opportunity to enhance existing in-car automation to aid the human driver in the undertaking of the driving task.

Also, the arguing machines were providing solely their output for purposes of ascertaining agreement versus disagreement. This is akin to the X and Y outputs that I've mentioned earlier herein.

Some setups for arguing machines do not have the machines actually carrying out an argument per se. In a manner similar to the famous Monty Python skit, the primary AI and the secondary AI are actually just differing in their outputs, perhaps you might say they are contradicting each other. Does the use of contradiction alone suffice to be an argument? The skit asked that same question.

In the case of true Level 5 self-driving cars, we are pursuing the circumstance of no human supervisor or human intervention to participate in the arbitration, along with the outputs of the AI instances being more robust, including too the presentation of their "arguments" for why their output should be considered the better of the choices provided to the arbitrator.

Removing the human supervisor accommodates the intent of true Level 5 self-driving cars. Making use of a more elaborated form of argument, beyond just the act of contradiction, will hopefully allow the arbitrator to make a more informed choice, doing so in lieu of resorting to asking a human to get involved.

When there is a disagreement, the more compelling argument will be given the nod as to the "winner" of which has the better output. There are various ways to quantify the measure of a compelling versus less compelling argument, which in our case involves the assignment of probabilities and uncertainties. This has to be done in a very time sensitive manner, and thus we are using templated structures that cover the main acts that the self-driving car would undertake while performing various driving tasks.

Conclusion

The use of AI arguing machines is a handy approach for dealing with real-time AI systems and provides a means to seek fail-safe operations involving life-and-death matters for humans. This is a somewhat newer and less-explored area of AI and still needs a lot of additional systematic study before it will be fully ready for prime time.

Nonetheless, I don't think there is much argument that AI arguing machines are well worth the attention of AI researchers and AI developers. Yes, it is. And if you say that no it is not, I'll repeat again that yes it is. And so on, we will go.

Lance B. Eliot

APPENDIX

Lance B. Eliot

APPENDIX A
TEACHING WITH THIS MATERIAL

The material in this book can be readily used either as a supplemental to other content for a class, or it can also be used as a core set of textbook material for a specialized class. Classes where this material is most likely used include any classes at the college or university level that want to augment the class by offering thought provoking and educational essays about AI and self-driving cars.

In particular, here are some aspects for class use:

o   Computer Science. Studying AI, autonomous vehicles, etc.

o   Business. Exploring technology and it adoption for business.

o   Sociology. Sociological views on the adoption and advancement of technology.

Specialized classes at the undergraduate and graduate level can also make use of this material.

For each chapter, consider whether you think the chapter provides material relevant to your course topic. There is plenty of opportunity to get the students thinking about the topic and force them to decide whether they agree or disagree with the points offered and positions taken. I would also encourage you to have the students do additional research beyond the chapter material presented (I provide next some suggested assignments they can do).

RESEARCH ASSIGNMENTS ON THESE TOPICS

Your students can find background material on these topics, doing so in various business and technical publications. I list below the top ranked AI related journals. For business publications, I would suggest the usual culprits such as the Harvard Business Review, Forbes, Fortune, WSJ, and the like.

Here are some suggestions of homework or projects that you could assign to students:

a) <u>Assignment for foundational AI research topic</u>: Research and prepare a paper and a presentation on a specific aspect of Deep AI, Machine Learning, ANN, etc. The paper should cite at least 3 reputable sources. Compare and contrast to what has been stated in this book.

b) <u>Assignment for the Self-Driving Car topic</u>: Research and prepare a paper and Self-Driving Cars. Cite at least 3 reputable sources and analyze the characterizations. Compare and contrast to what has been stated in this book.

c) <u>Assignment for a Business topic</u>: Research and prepare a paper and a presentation on businesses and advanced technology. What is hot, and what is not? Cite at least 3 reputable sources. Compare and contrast to the depictions in this book.

d) <u>Assignment to do a Startup:</u> Have the students prepare a paper about how they might startup a business in this realm. They must submit a sound Business Plan for the startup. They could also be asked to present their Business Plan and so should also have a presentation deck to coincide with it.

You can certainly adjust the aforementioned assignments to fit to your particular needs and the class structure. You'll notice that I ask for 3 reputable cited sources for the paper writing based assignments. I usually steer students toward "reputable" publications, since otherwise they will cite some oddball source that has no credentials other than that they happened to write something and post it onto the Internet. You can define "reputable" in whatever way you prefer, for example some faculty think Wikipedia is not reputable while others believe it is reputable and allow students to cite it.

The reason that I usually ask for at least 3 citations is that if the student only does one or two citations they usually settle on whatever they happened to find the fastest. By requiring three citations, it usually seems to force them to look around, explore, and end-up probably finding five or more, and then whittling it down to 3 that they will actually use.

I have not specified the length of their papers, and leave that to you to tell the students what you prefer. For each of those assignments, you could end-up with a short one to two pager, or you could do a dissertation length paper. Base the length on whatever best fits for your class, and the credit amount of the assignment within the context of the other grading metrics you'll be using for the class.

I mention in the assignments that they are to do a paper and prepare a presentation. I usually try to get students to present their work. This is a good practice for what they will do in the business world. Most of the time, they will be required to prepare an analysis and present it. If you don't have the class time or inclination to have the students present, then you can of course cut out the aspect of them putting together a presentation.

If you want to point students toward highly ranked journals in AI, here's a list of the top journals as reported by *various citation counts sources* (this list changes year to year):

o   Communications of the ACM

o   Artificial Intelligence

o   Cognitive Science

o   IEEE Transactions on Pattern Analysis and Machine Intelligence

o   Foundations and Trends in Machine Learning

o   Journal of Memory and Language

o   Cognitive Psychology

o   Neural Networks

o   IEEE Transactions on Neural Networks and Learning Systems

o   IEEE Intelligent Systems

o   Knowledge-based Systems

GUIDE TO USING THE CHAPTERS

For each of the chapters, I provide next some various ways to use the chapter material. You can assign the tasks as individual homework assignments, or the tasks can be used with team projects for the class. You can easily layout a series of assignments, such as indicating that the students are to do item "a" below for say Chapter 1, then "b" for the next chapter of the book, and so on.

a) What is the main point of the chapter and describe in your own words the significance of the topic,

b) Identify at least two aspects in the chapter that you agree with, and support your concurrence by providing at least one other outside researched item as support; make sure to explain your basis for disagreeing with the aspects,

c) Identify at least two aspects in the chapter that you disagree with, and support your disagreement by providing at least one other outside researched item as support; make sure to explain your basis for disagreeing with the aspects,

d) Find an aspect that was not covered in the chapter, doing so by conducting outside research, and then explain how that aspect ties into the chapter and what significance it brings to the topic,

e) Interview a specialist in industry about the topic of the chapter, collect from them their thoughts and opinions, and readdress the chapter by citing your source and how they compared and contrasted to the material,

f) Interview a relevant academic professor or researcher in a college or university about the topic of the chapter, collect from them their thoughts and opinions, and readdress the chapter by citing your source and how they compared and contrasted to the material,

g) Try to update a chapter by finding out the latest on the topic, and ascertain whether the issue or topic has now been solved or whether it is still being addressed, explain what you come up with.

The above are all ways in which you can get the students of your class involved in considering the material of a given chapter. You could mix things up by having one of those above assignments per each week, covering the chapters over the course of the semester or quarter.

As a reminder, here are the chapters of the book and you can select whichever chapters you find most valued for your particular class:

<u>Chapter Title</u>

Companion Book By This Author

Advances in AI and Autonomous Vehicles: Cybernetic Self-Driving Cars

Practical Advances in Artificial Intelligence (AI) and Machine Learning

by

Dr. Lance B. Eliot, MBA, PhD

This title is available via Amazon and other book sellers

Companion Book By This Author

Self-Driving Cars:
"The Mother of All AI Projects"

by Dr. Lance B. Eliot, MBA, PhD

This title is available via Amazon and other book sellers

Companion Book By This Author

Innovation and Thought Leadership on Self-Driving Driverless Cars

by Dr. Lance B. Eliot, MBA, PhD

This title is available via Amazon and other book sellers

<u>Companion Book By This Author</u>

New Advances in AI Autonomous Driverless Cars Self-Driving Cars

by Dr. Lance B. Eliot, MBA, PhD

<u>Chapter Title</u>

This title is available via Amazon and other book sellers

Companion Book By This Author

Introduction to
Driverless Self-Driving Cars

by Dr. Lance B. Eliot, MBA, PhD

Chapter Title

This title is available via Amazon and other book sellers

Lance B. Eliot

Companion Book By This Author

Autonomous Vehicle Driverless Self-Driving Cars and Artificial Intelligence

by Dr. Lance B. Eliot, MBA, PhD

This title is available via Amazon and other book sellers

Lance B. Eliot

Companion Book By This Author

Transformative Artificial Intelligence Driverless Self-Driving Cars

by Dr. Lance B. Eliot, MBA, PhD

This title is available via Amazon and other book sellers

Lance B. Eliot

This title is available via Amazon and other book sellers

Companion Book By This Author

State-of-the-Art
AI Driverless Self-Driving Cars

by Dr. Lance B. Eliot, MBA, PhD

Chapter Title

This title is available via Amazon and other book sellers

Companion Book By This Author

Top Trends in
AI Self-Driving Cars

by Dr. Lance B. Eliot, MBA, PhD

This title is available via Amazon and other book sellers

Companion Book By This Author

AI Innovations and Self-Driving Cars

by Dr. Lance B. Eliot, MBA, PhD

This title is available via Amazon and other book sellers

Companion Book By This Author

Crucial Advances for
AI Self-Driving Cars

by Dr. Lance B. Eliot, MBA, PhD

This title is available via Amazon and other book sellers

Lance B. Eliot

Companion Book By This Author

Sociotechnical Insights and AI Driverless Cars

by Dr. Lance B. Eliot, MBA, PhD

Chapter Title

This title is available via Amazon and other book sellers

Lance B. Eliot

<u>Companion Book By This Author</u>

Pioneering Advances for AI Driverless Cars

by Dr. Lance B. Eliot, MBA, PhD

This title is available via Amazon and other book sellers

Leading Edge Trends for AI Driverless Cars

by Dr. Lance B. Eliot, MBA, PhD

This title is available via Amazon and other book sellers

Companion Book By This Author

The Cutting Edge of
AI Autonomous Cars

by Dr. Lance B. Eliot, MBA, PhD

This title is available via Amazon and other book sellers

Companion Book By This Author

The Next Wave of
AI Self-Driving Cars

by Dr. Lance B. Eliot, MBA, PhD

This title is available via Amazon and other book sellers

Lance B. Eliot

<u>Companion Book By This Author</u>

Revolutionary Innovations of AI Self-Driving Cars

by Dr. Lance B. Eliot, MBA, PhD

<u>Chapter Title</u>

This title is available via Amazon and other book sellers

Lance B. Eliot

ABOUT THE AUTHOR

Dr. Lance B. Eliot, MBA, PhD is the CEO of Techbruim, Inc. and Executive Director of the Cybernetic AI Self-Driving Car Institute, and has over twenty years of industry experience including serving as a corporate officer in a billion dollar firm and was a partner in a major executive services firm. He is also a serial entrepreneur having founded, ran, and sold several high-tech related businesses. He previously hosted the popular radio show *Technotrends* that was also available on American Airlines flights via their in-flight audio program. Author or co-author of a dozen books and over 400 articles, he has made appearances on CNN, and has been a frequent speaker at industry conferences.

A former professor at the University of Southern California (USC), he founded and led an innovative research lab on Artificial Intelligence in Business. Known as the "AI Insider" his writings on AI advances and trends has been widely read and cited. He also previously served on the faculty of the University of California Los Angeles (UCLA), and was a visiting professor at other major universities. He was elected to the International Board of the Society for Information Management (SIM), a prestigious association of over 3,000 high-tech executives worldwide.

He has performed extensive community service, including serving as Senior Science Adviser to the Vice Chair of the Congressional Committee on Science & Technology. He has served on the Board of the OC Science & Engineering Fair (OCSEF), where he is also has been a Grand Sweepstakes judge, and likewise served as a judge for the Intel International SEF (ISEF). He served as the Vice Chair of the Association for Computing Machinery (ACM) Chapter, a prestigious association of computer scientists. Dr. Eliot has been a shark tank judge for the USC Mark Stevens Center for Innovation on start-up pitch competitions, and served as a mentor for several incubators and accelerators in Silicon Valley and Silicon Beach. He served on several Boards and Committees at USC, including having served on the Marshall Alumni Association (MAA) Board in Southern California.

Dr. Eliot holds a PhD from USC, MBA, and Bachelor's in Computer Science, and earned the CDP, CCP, CSP, CDE, and CISA certifications. Born and raised in Southern California, and having traveled and lived internationally, he enjoys scuba diving, surfing, and sailing.

ADDENDUM

Revolutionary Innovations of AI Driverless Cars

Practical Advances in Artificial Intelligence (AI) and Machine Learning

By

Dr. Lance B. Eliot, MBA, PhD

———

For supplemental materials of this book, visit:

www.ai-selfdriving-cars.guru

For special orders of this book, contact:

LBE Press Publishing

Email: LBE.Press.Publishing@gmail.com

www.ingramcontent.com/pod-product-compliance
Lightning Source LLC
Chambersburg PA
CBHW031553280326
41928CB00047BA/215